MEDIA MANUALS

MEDIA MANUALS

TV CAMERA OPERATION
Gerald Millerson

BASIC TV STAGING
Gerald Millerson

THE USE OF MICROPHONES
Alec Nisbett

YOUR FILM & THE LAB
L. Bernard Happé

TV SOUND OPERATIONS
Glyn Alkin

TV LIGHTING METHODS
Gerald Millerson

16mm FILM CUTTING
John Burder

THE SMALL TV STUDIO
Alan Bermingham, Michael Talbot-Smith,
John Symons, & Ken Angold-Stephens.

Forthcoming titles
Using Videotape
Sound Recording & Reproduction
The Lens in Action
The Lens & All Its Jobs
Timing for Animation
Motion Picture Camera – Choice & Technique
The Rostrum Camera
The Practice of TV Production
Basic Film Technique

16 mm
Film
Cutting

John
Burder

A Focal Press Book

Communication Arts Books
HASTINGS HOUSE, PUBLISHERS
New York, NY 10016

ISBN 8038 - 6730 - 1 (Text Edition)

Library of Congress Catalog Card Number: 75 - 6057

Printed and bound in Great Britain by Staples Printers Ltd., Kettering, Northants.

Contents

6

Introduction

This is a practical book for learning how to cut 16mm films for television and for other outlets. The book is based on cutting techniques used by the BBC and by most other major television networks. I have adopted the points made in the text to teach many people in the past how to cut 16mm films and, indeed, have used the same techniques myself for a number of years to cut films of every type.

I have placed little emphasis on paperwork but much more on practicalities. Cutting is a practical job and much must be learned by practice. An editor often has to work under pressure and at speed. The book starts with a look at the equipment to be found in a cutting room and then goes on to show how to cut the action of a film from rushes to show print. Laboratory processes are explored and also the preparation of soundtracks for films shot with sound and for those shot without any sound at all. Finally, we see how copies of the cut film can be produced.

I am most grateful to Lesley Chubb who has typed the manuscript for me and to the BBC who originally taught me how to cut. I am also indebted to Sorel Films who have enabled me to find time to work on this book. I would also like to thank Paul Petzold who has been so helpful in adapting my manuscript to fit the format of this series and to Percy Poynter who has translated my rough sketches into drawings which are clear and easy to follow.

Cutting is an important and a fascinating job but before the creative possibilities of cutting can be enjoyed, basic techniques must be mastered. This book is designed to provide a sound basis for further practical experiments.

John Burder

The Job of Cutting

The editor is responsible for the film from the time the processed camera original is printed to the time the final edited version of the film is shown to an audience. He combines artistry and technique and gives the film a definite pace. His job starts when the film has been shot and processed. Few films are shot in the order in which scenes occur in the finished film and many scenes are photographed more than once, so the editor's first job is to sort out the right scenes and the best takes and assemble them in script order. He then fine cuts the assembly, cutting from scene to scene at the most advantageous points. When the film is completed audiences will hear only one sound track but in the cutting room a number of different tracks must be prepared — for music, dialogue and sound effects. The tracks must all be cut to match the edited version of the picture. They can then be mixed together in a dubbing theatre to make the final composite track audiences will hear on the finished film.

Importance of cutting
Cutting is one of the most important parts of the whole film making process. If a film has been well shot all the efforts of the camera team can be wasted if the editor puts the scenes together inefficiently. On the other hand, a film shot adequately but without any particular distinction can often be improved by skilful cutting.

What do you cut?
When the film is shot, film exposed in the camera is sent each day to a laboratory for processing. The laboratory processes the original film and makes a rush print: a copy for cutting purposes. In the U.S.A. these first prints are known as 'dailies'. Elsewhere the term 'rushes' is more widely used. The camera original remains uncut until the final shape and form of each sequence has been determined. Then you can match the camera original to the work print. You can then make further copies from the matched original — copies which will be free of the dirt, scratches and joins found in the cutting copy.

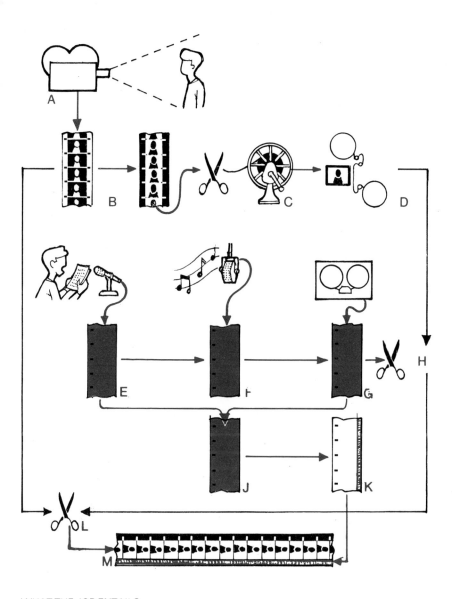

WHAT THE JOB ENTAILS

Cutting programme
Shoot (A). Process the original film and make a copy for cutting (B).
Assemble (C) then fine cut (D). Separate soundtracks of narration (E) Music
(F) and sound effects (G) can then be recorded on perforated magnetic film.
Cut the tracks to match the picture (H). Mix the tracks together (dub) (J). Re-
record the final mix soundtrack as an optical sound negative (K). Match the
uncut original to the edited cutting copy (L). Print the original with the sound
neg to make comopt sound prints ready for showing (M).

Cutting with Safety and Economy

Why not cut the original film exposed in the camera? The simple answer is that it is too valuable. In the course of cutting any film you will find you need to experiment with the shape and form of some of the sequences. When you start cutting you will know the sort of film you want to end up with, but when you actually come to put scenes together you will find you need to experiment. You may wish to try a sequence first one way and then in a different form. Now, if you are cutting a work print, alterations will not present any problem. You can cut the copy and change it as often as you like. If everything goes wrong you can always go back to the camera original and make another print. In the course of cutting, the work print will get worn and scratched. That does not matter either, but if the camera original were to become scratched or worn it would be a disaster for the damage would be reproduced on every copy printed from it. When the edited work print has been perfected the camera original can be matched to the edited print.

Matching original to cutting copy
This matching process is known as negative cutting. It is a specialist job usually undertaken by a technician working at it full time. Neg cutters match the original to the edited copy by comparing a series of numbers on the side of the film. These numbers are printed on the edge of the original film exposed in the camera and, when a copy is produced, they are also present in that. It is simply a case of matching number to number. When original and copy match each other exactly, a laboratory can produce show copies of the edited version of the film by printing the matched original on a reel of new stock, free of joins.

A chance to save money
If you are working on a tight budget, there is one early stage of production where you can sometimes save money. If the film you are cutting has been shot in colour it is quite possible to make a black and white cutting copy from the colour original. The method for doing this is shown on page 48. When a colour film is cut in black and white it is always worth printing at least one roll in colour to check the quality. It is also worth asking the processing laboratory to print the cutting copy on panchromatic stock. Pan stocks are sensitive to all the colours of the spectrum and will thus show up any edge fogging which could get lost on other printing stocks.

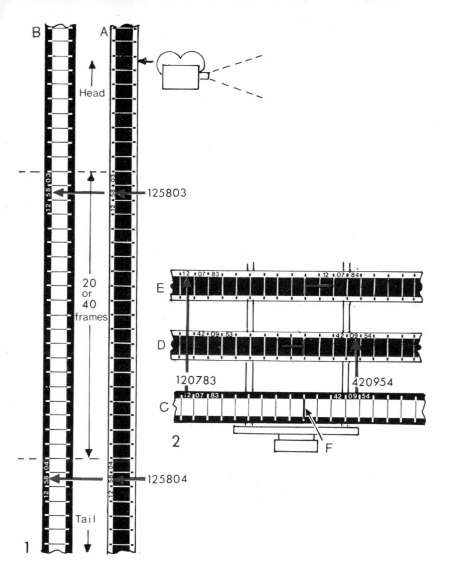

THE COPY YOU CUT

1. Edge numbers

When a camera original film (A) is printed (B) the edge numbers on the
original will be reproduced on the copy. You will find one edge number in
every 40, or sometimes every 20 frames.

2. Cutting by numbers

The cutting copy in a synchroniser (C) has been cut at F. The uncut originals
of the outgoing and incoming scenes (D & E) have been put alongside ready
for neg-cutting. When original and cutting copy are matched the neg cutter
matches the edge numbers and then cuts at the point indicated.

13

Cutting Films Shot with Sound

When you cut a film you cut picture and sound. The sound may be recorded when the film is photographed or may be added later in the cutting room. A film may be shot with sound synchronised with the action. Alternatively it may be shot without any sound at all, or with 'wild' tracks. When you cut a film you will also be responsible for preparing the final film soundtrack.

Cutting programme — synchronised sound

If the film has ben shot with synchronised sound you will be handling soundtracks throughout the cutting process. When 16mm synchronised sound scenes are filmed, the action is normally photographed on 'mute' film stock while the sound is simultaneously recorded on quarter inch tape, on equipment electronically locked to the camera by a synchronising pulse in order to keep in step with it. At the end of each day's filming, the mute camera original is sent to a laboratory for processing and for a copy for cutting to be produced. The original sound recording must also be copied and should be sent to a sound recording studio where it can be re-recorded on perforated magnetic film. You will then receive the picture rushes and the perforated magnetic film sound copy in the cutting room. Your first job will be to synchronise the two separate strips of film: the sound and picture. Then you can cut sound and picture, making a first assembly and, after that, a fine cut.

Completing the soundtrack

It is extremely unlikely that all scenes will be photographed with synchronised sound. In the course of editing you will prepare several different soundtracks, all matching the one reel of edited picture material. Some soundtracks will contain the sounds recorded when the film was photographed. Other tracks will be needed to fill in the background sounds and the scenes which have not been photographed with synchronised sound. You will have to prepare these tracks in the course of cutting. When they have been prepared you can mix all your tracks together in a dubbing theatre and make the final mix soundtrack audiences will hear on the finished film. Then you can match the camera original to your edited cutting copy and make prints of sound and picture.

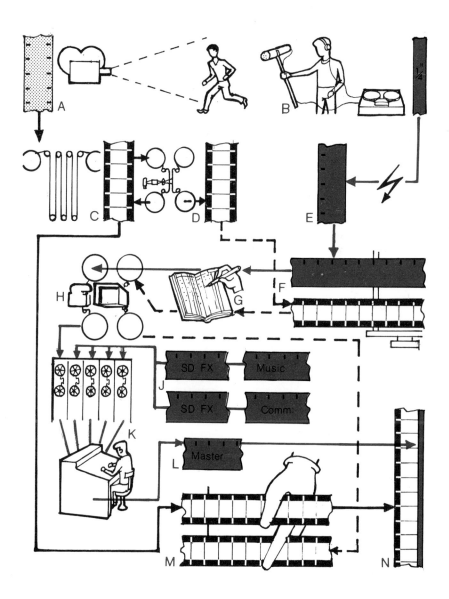

CUTTING FILMS SHOT WITH SYNC. SOUND

Production programme

Shoot on mute film stock (A) record on $\frac{1}{4}$in tape (B). Process the original film (C) and print a cutting copy (D). Re-record taped location sound on perforated magnetic film (E). Synchronise sound and picture rushes (F). Log (G). Assemble and fine cut (H). Prepare additional soundtrack (J). Dub (K) to make final mix master soundtrack (L). Match camera original and cutting copy (M). Print sound and picture together to make copies for showing (N).

Cutting Films Shot Without Sound

Sound films in 16mm are quite often shot without any sound recording being made simultaneously. Many documentary films are shot without sound and the whole work of preparing a soundtrack is done in the cutting room. If you are cutting this kind of film the main stages of the job will be as follows:

1. Shoot film.
2. Process original and print cutting copy
3. Log rushes.
4. Break down rushes and assemble in script order.
5. Fine cut picture.
6. Re-record tape and disc sound effects and music on perforated magnetic film.
7. Record narration.
8. Match narration and sound effects tracks to fine cut picture.
9. Dub final sound.
10. Neg cut.
11. Produce copies for showing.

You start by editing the picture in the normal way. Then you can think about sound. Look at your edited cutting copy and analyse it in terms of sound. Make a list of the sounds (music and effects) you need for each scene. You can then choose suitable tapes or discs of the sounds from a sound library and arrange for them to be re-recorded on perforated magnetic film. Next you must match sound and picture. In doing this you will build up a series of different soundtracks all matching your one cut reel of picture. If the film has a commentary you can record it at this stage, again recording on perforated magnetic film. The narration can then be matched to the edited picture. This is the most precise way of recording narration for it enables you to match sound and picture exactly. An alternative, not so precise, is to record during the final dub. When you have prepared all the soundtracks needed to bring the scenes to life you can dub the final mix. Then it is simply a case of matching the camera original to the edited cutting copy and making copies for showing.

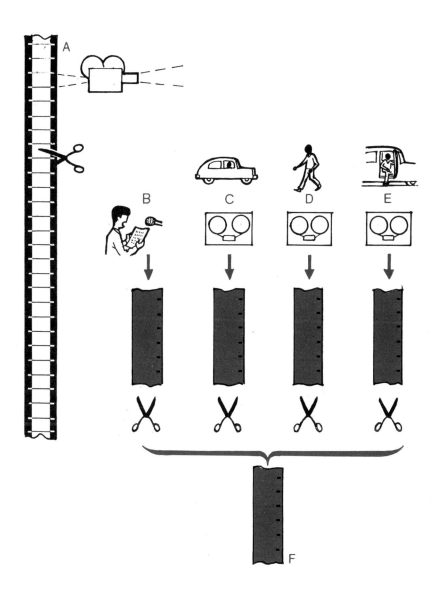

CUTTING SOUND FILMS SHOT 'MUTE'

Building up a soundtrack

Shoot (A), make a copy and cut. Record voice over narration (B). Transfer
sound effects (C, D & E) from tape or disc to perforated magnetic film. Cut
with cutting copy action. Dub to make final composite track — the final mix
master (F).

Motorised Editing Machines

When you cut your film you will want to be able to run it at the speed at which audiences will see the finished film projected. You could use a projector to check with, but you cannot employ it as a viewer for the cutting process because the machine is not built to stand up to constant stopping and starting. The necessary performance is provided by special machine designed also to serve the various functions required in editing.

Machines for sound and picture

An editing machine must produce a picture which is clear, reasonably steady and large enough to show details like footsteps and lip movements, all of which can be extremely important when cutting sound sequences. It must be able to stop on a particular frame and to run at variable speeds and constant speed (24 fps, or 25 for some television studios) forwards and in reverse. It must run at normal speed in order to assess the pace of the film and the timing of the cuts so that they can be accurate to a frame. When you have seen your cutting copy a hundred times and need to run through the whole film to make adjustments to the end you will appreciate the advantage of being able to run at double speed. Should you want to check a slight but critical movement or the precise point of a cut you will appreciate being able to inch the picture frame by frame, so variable speed control is essential.

Cutting sound and picture

The machine must also be able to project sound and picture in synchronism or independently. Most power operated editing machines will project one reel of picture and one or more sound tracks recorded on perforated magnetic film. Some combine 16mm picture with 35mm sound tracks. A few years ago, because many dubbing theatres were only equipped to run 35mm sound, 16mm films were often cut with 35mm tracks. Today a motorised editing machine should be able to run 16mm picture with at least one track of 16mm sound.

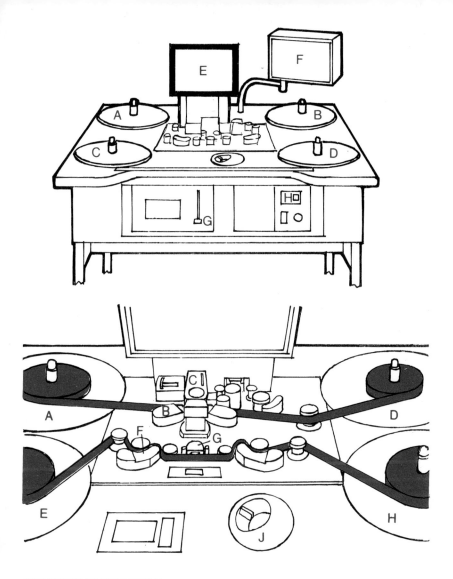

STEENBECK EDITING TABLE

1. 16 mm Four plate model

Picture feed plate (A) and take up plate (B) sound feed plate (C) and take up (D) are set above the main on/off controls (H) and a volume control (G) the picture is back projected on an eye level screen (E) with loudspeaker alongside (F).

2. Lacing path and direction control

Picture (A) passes via a drive sprocket (B) through the picture gate (C) where a rotating prism back-projects on the screen above and on to the picture take up plate (D). Magnetic sound (E) passes via a drive sprocket (F) over the magnetic sound head (G) to take up (H). One lever (J) operates variable speed forward and reverse direction controls.

19

Upright and Table Editing Machines

Editing machines meeting these requirements can be divided into two main groups — upright machines like the Moviola, and table machines like the Steenbeck.

Upright machines: Moviola
The Hollywood Moviola is perhaps the oldest established editing machine. The word Moviola is a trade name, the name of an American editing machine. It is so widely used in the U.S.A. however, that it is now almost the generic term for any kind of motorised editing machine. The standard Moviola is in international use. There are several different models but for 16mm work one combining 16mm picture and 16mm sound is probably most suitable. The picture on a Moviola is driven by an intermittent sprocket with loops above and below the picture gate. The screen is not large but the picture is bright and the machine is ideal for running short lengths of film. It can be controlled by hand, switch or by footpedal and sound and picture can be run together in synchronism or independently. There is provision for running from reel to reel but I have always found this machine far more suitable for running individual film shots than for continuous projection. These are good machines to work with, though today many editors prefer to use a flat editing table.

Table editing machines: Steenbeck
In a table editing machine, picture and sound pass from left to right, horizontally. Table machines are quick and simple to use. They take very little time to lace up and the quality of sound and picture is frequently excellent. One of the best machines is made by the German Steenbeck company. Again, this firm makes a number of different models but for 16mm cutting the ST600W, four plate machine is ideal. The layout is simple, the operation easy to control and the performance excellent. Sound and picture can be projected together or separately at normal or double speeds, forward or in reverse. All the direction movements are controlled by one lever which enables you to run at speeds between two and a hundred frames per second. The picture is back projected on a screen measuring 18 x 25cm and the cold light source used for illumination gives a bright picture and long lamp life. A film footage counter or minute/second counter is located near the picture gate. The basic ST600W machine is designed to run one reel of sound with one reel of picture but other models are available one of which combines 16mm picture with two tracks of sound.

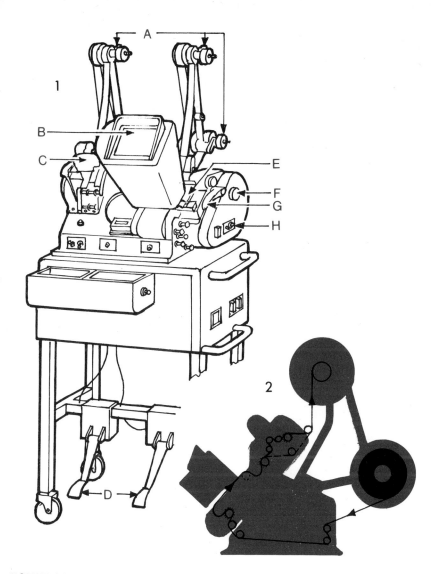

HOLLYWOOD MOVIOLA

1. Layout and controls

Film passes from feed spindles (A) to take up with sound running on the left via soundhead (C) and picture on the right where it is projected on a screen (B). The screen can be moved to give access to the film by releasing locking catch (E). A brake for instant stopping (G) picture and motor on/off switches (H) and a picture head motor rheostat control are all on the right. Film direction and speed control pedals (D).

2. Film lacing path

Picture film passes from top to bottom via two feed sprockets and a loop (9-10 frames) to the picture gate. Another 9-10 frame loop after the picture gate leads the film via a further feed sprocket to the take up.

Low Cost & Versatile Editing Equipment

The machines discussed so far can all be used satisfactorily for 16mm cutting. You may find that you have to use a machine of a type other than those mentioned which are reliable, but tend to be expensive. A number of low cost machines are also available. Some are reliable, many are not and, if you are thinking of buying 16mm cutting equipment it is important to remember this when making your choice. Motorised editing machines have to withstand considerable wear and tear and they need to be sturdily built. Some low cost machines are more expensive to keep in repair than they are to buy in the first place. Always choose a machine suitable for the sort of work you are planning to do. A small low cost machine may be perfectly adequate for limited editing work but with long hours of hard use it may soon prove inadequate.

Acmade Miniola
One of the more realiable low cost machines is the Acmade Miniola. Its performance should not be compared with the other products we have discussed for it is far cheaper. It is an upright editing machine working on the same basic principles as those previously mentioned. The Miniola will run one reel of film and also one soundtrack. Sound and picture can be projected at normal or double speeds in synchronism or independently. the film paths run parellel with the picture running above the soundtrack. the picture is back projected on a small screen and the take up and feed plates all take up to 2,000 ft. of 16mm film.

Prevost and Kem
The Italian Prevost company also make a wide range of editing tables. They are rugged but tend to be rather complicated to lace up — which can waste time when cutting. Kem machines are built on a modular principle so that it is possible to switch from one gauge to another with the minimum of fuss. A 16mm machine can be converted to 35mm by slotting out one unit and slotting in another. Again, there are a number of models available capable of running different combinations of picture and sound. One of the larger Kem tables can run three separate 16mm pictures and two tracks. Another machine will run one picture and three tracks. For normal cutting purposes one reel of picture and one reel of track will sufflce.

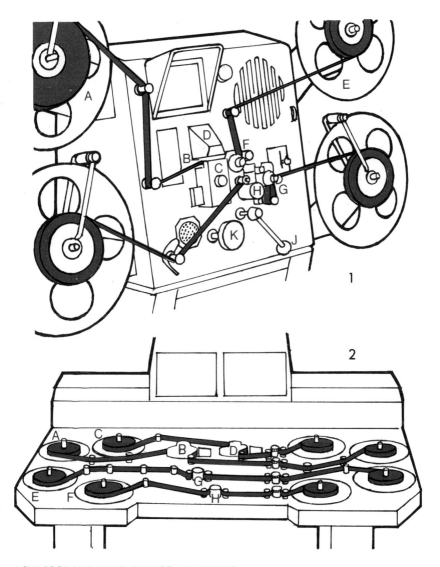

LOW COST AND MULTI-PURPOSE MACHINES

1. Acmade Miniola
Picture (A) runs via picture gate (B) where light from lamphouse (C) shines
through the film and via a prism (D) on to the screen. A single drive sprocket
(F) moves the film. Sound is also driven by one sprocket (G) over soundhead
(H). Lever (J) controls forward and reverse running and there is an inching
knob (K).

2. Prevost. Eight-plate two-picture two-track machine
Picture 1 (A) and picture 2 (C) run via projection heads (B and D).
Soundtracks (E and F) run via soundheads (G and H).

23

Synchronisers: Types and Uses

Like motorised editing machines, synchronisers are vital pieces of cutting room equipment. The synchroniser, which is sometimes called the gang synchroniser, is a device for keeping the picture and a number of soundtracks in synchronism on the cutting bench.

The bench is easy to identify because it will normally have two linen bags hanging underneath. Between the two bags is a square glass panel set into the surface of the bench. A light is positioned under the glass panel and the synchroniser is normally used on this panel so that light shines through the film. The top of editing benches should be covered with plastic laminate or something as tough and easy to keep clean. It should not be longer than 60in and about 24in deep. It is a good idea to have either a film cuts rack (see list of accessories) or racks for holding small reels of film trims behind the editing bench. On the top of the bench, as well as the synchroniser you will always find at least one rewind arm and possibly a film horse but the central and most important piece of equipment will always be a synchroniser.

Gang synchronisers

A synchroniser has two or more sprockets locked on a common shaft which holds picture and sound in perfect synchronism, even when moved. The film is held on the sprockets by sprung rollers which can be raised to place the film on the sprocket teeth, then lowered and locked to hold it in position. Once the film is locked on the sprocket teeth it will remain synchronised which ever way the sprockets turn. The main shaft turns on sealed ball-bearings and synchronisers generally need little maintenance though they must be kept clean at all times. Like the editing machine, there are several different models to choose from. The two main kinds of synchroniser are the standard type and picture synchronisers. Both types are available in a number of different models.

Synchronisers are available in 16mm two-way and four-way models, and combination 16mm/35mm synchronisers are also quite common. The four-way synchroniser (also known as the four gang synchroniser) has four separate sprockets locked to a common shaft and the two-way has, naturally, two. The four-way is widely used when preparing soundtracks and for negative cutting.

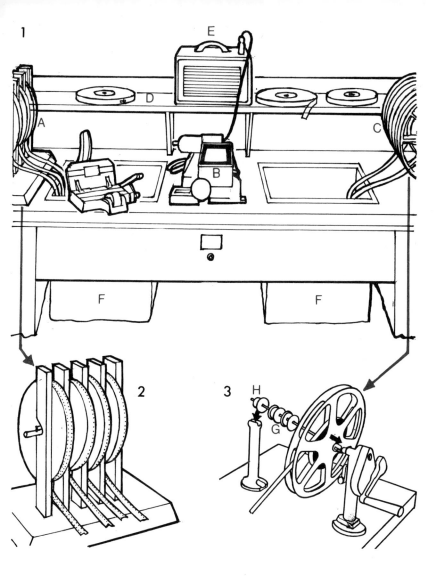

THE CUTTING BENCH

. On the left of the bench a film horse (A) holds film on cores. Synchroniser (B) and amplifier (E) are used throughout cutting. Reels of spacing (D) will also be needed. Cloth bags (F) enable film to be wound back and forth through the synchroniser without using take up (C) until adjustments have been completed.

2. 16mm four way film horse

3. Sych. bench take up arm
Reels are separated from each other by small springs (G) and held in position by a single clamp (H) Four reels can be fitted on one arm.

Synchronisers: Accessories

Various attachments are available to extend the usefulness of a standard bench synchroniser.

Sound attachments for synchronisers

Many synchronisers have small magnetic soundheads attached to the second and subsequent sprockets. The front sprocket is normally used for picture and thus does not have a sound head attached to it. Instead, individual frame numbers are frequently marked on the leading edge of the front sprocket. The output of the magnetic heads attached to the other sprockets can be connected to a small amplifier and loudspeaker unit. Sound recorded on the various tracks used in the synchroniser can then be heard. The sound heads are used when synchronising rushes (see page 120) and when preparing a series of soundtracks.

Picture synchroniser

On standard gang synchronisers the only way of seeing the picture is to stop the motion of the synchroniser and examine the film with the aid of light from the glass panel under the synchroniser. "Picture" synchronisers have a small viewing screen above the front sprocket so that you can see a projected picture from the film placed in the front sprocket. These picture synchronisers are now coming into wide general use. Once you have used one you will find it quite indispensible.

Synchroniser accessories and attachments

Film footage and sometimes frame counters are standard fittings on synchronisers of all kinds. Though there are firms making motor attachments, synchronisers are perhaps best propelled by hand or driven by taking up slack film on reels placed on the right hand side of the synchroniser and gradually increasing the tension of the film until the wheels of the synchroniser begin to move. Motor drive units are available but as most of them drive the synchroniser and not the feed- and take-up reels their uses are limited. With practice you will find you can cut a film on a synchroniser alone. In television studios, where programmes often have to be produced against a very tight time schedule, there is sometimes no alternative.

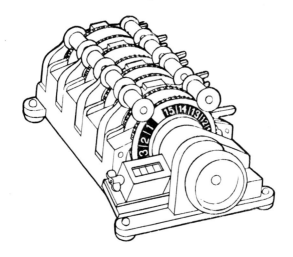

1

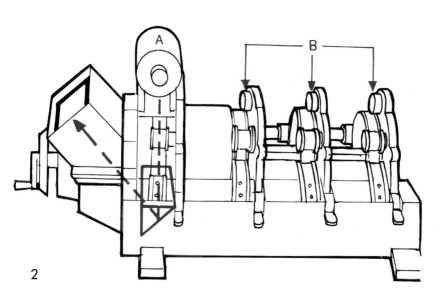

2

SYNCHRONISERS

1. Four way gang synchroniser
Designed to hold four strips of film in synchronism. A footage or frame counter is standard equipment.

2. Four way picture synchroniser
Picture, in the front track, is illuminated by a small lamp (A) which shines through the film via a prism to a small screen. The lamphouse can be moved so that you can mark the film. Small magnetic soundheads are frequently set into the other tracks (B).

27

Joining Film: Temporary Splices

The item of cutting room equipment you will use most will be the film joiner or splicer as it is often called. The process of making a join will be discussed later together with cutting techniques for picture (Pages 56 and 64). At this stage we will simply describe the types of film joiner you will find in a cutting room. Film can be joined with tape or with cement. Tape joins are essentially temporary. Cement joins are permanent. Both types are widely used and you must know how to operate joiners of both kinds.

Temporary joins: tape splicers

For cutting copy dry splicers using tape are ideal. The best known and most widely used is made in Italy by the Incollatrici company. It uses ordinary clear tape which is easy to obtain and makes a strong join in a matter of seconds. The important point about tape joiners is the type of tape they use. The Incollatrici uses ordinary unperforated tape. You lay the two pieces of film to be joined end to end on the joiner block and draw the tape across. You then lower a cutting handle which presses the tape onto the film and punches out the sprocket holes, thus making the ordinary tape into tape with 16mm perforations so that the joined film will run happily through film equipment. This is a speedy and economic method. Some other tape joiners need pre-perforated tape to operate. The tape must be perforated before the film is joined. You still cut and place the film to be joined on the joiner block but you then have to line up the perforations on the pre-perforated tape with the sprocket holes of the film. Some machines I have seen are so badly designed that this alignment is a time consuming job and a very difficult one to do satisfactorily. Moreover, pre-perforated tape tends to be expensive. So, if you are thinking of buying a new joiner examine the costs carefully. The method of joining with tape on an Incollatrici joiner is discussed on page 56.

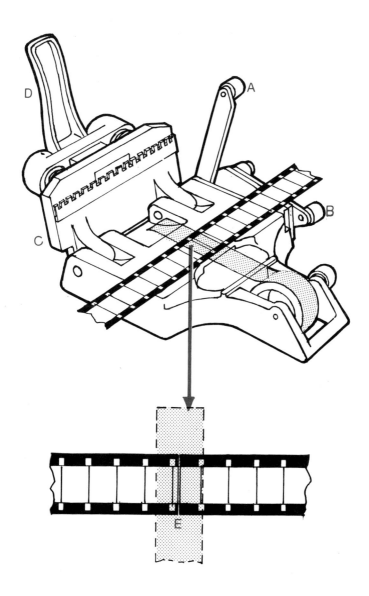

JOINING WITH TAPE

Incollatrici tape joiner

First cut your film with the straight cutter (A) for picture or the diagonal one
(B) for magnetic. Lay the two scenes to be joined end to end on the joiner
block and pull-tape across (E). Close top of joiner (C) and press down handle
(D) to punch out sprocket holes and cut tape.

29

Joining Films: Permanent Splices

The alternative to joining with tape is to use a liquid solution known as film cement. Cement splicers, like tape joiners, are available in several different forms. Tape joins are ideal for cutting copy use. Cement splicers are suitable for joining original film and show prints. Tape discolours with age and many laboratory film printing machines cannot cope with tape joins. When you join with tape you lay the two pieces of film to be joined end to end on the joining black without an overlap. When you join with cement you need an overlap. To join two pieces of film together the emulsion must be scraped off the overlapping edge of the film. Cement can then be applied to the edge and the two pieces of film clamped together. The cement actually welds the pieces of film to one another. On some types of cement splicer heat is applied to the area being joined. This tends to produce a stronger join and also reduces the time that film needs to be left in the joiner. The minimum overlap used for 16mm film is 1/16in. This minimal width should be used when joining camera originals or any kind of master film. It is vitally important to keep cement joiners clean and in alignment, and to avoid using an excessive amount of cement. A wet splice can easily intrude into the picture area. The correct technique for joining with a cement joiner is discussed on page 58.

Welded splices
Another type of joiner producing a heat butt welded splice is often used by negative cutters. The film is not overlapped for the splicer cuts along the frame line and joins the two pieces together by welding along the joint. The welded splice is very strong. You do not need to scrape off the emulsion or apply cement and no frames are lost and there is much to recommend this kind of join when negative cutting original film. For the cutting copy, tape joins are better for they enable you to alter a cut with the minimum of fuss. It is almost impossible to peel or alter a welded butt join.

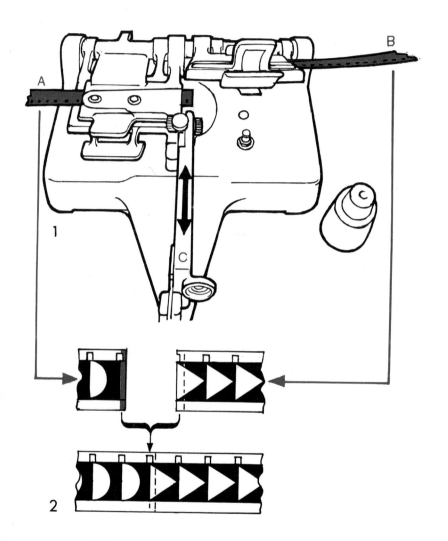

JOINING WITH CEMENT

Overlap splice

The two scenes to be joined (A & B) are brought into contact with each other
after the overlapping edge on the left has been scraped clear of emulsion by a
scraper (C). The overlapping area can be seen in the finished join (2).

Animated Viewers

Some cutting rooms are equipped with an animated viewer. Amateur movie makers frequently do all their editing on a viewer of this kind which they call an 'editor'. Animated viewers usually consist of a few rollers and a small viewing screen, three or four inches across, on which the picture is projected via a rotating prism. They are often fixed to a small baseboard with a rewind arm on either side. To move the frames through the gate you increase the tension on the film, which is fed from one rewind arm to the other via the viewer. The speed at which film can be viewed depends entirely on the speed at which the rewind arms are turned. This kind of viewer can be useful in finding material to make a first assembly but its professional applications are strictly limited. The main reason for the limitation is that as the rewind arms are not power operated but controlled by hand, the speed at which film passes through the machine will vary depending on the amount of effort applied. It is thus impossible to gauge the exact effect of any shot duration accurately.

Function of the Viewer in cutting

Two particular makes of viewer are sometimes found in cutting rooms. The Zeiss Moviscop and the Muray viewer are both quite widely used. The Muray is one of the cheaper viewers and gives excellent performance. It is made from metal, is reasonably sturdy and gives a good bright picture on a ground glass screen. The film passes under two guide rollers, the second of which holds the film on a sprocket. This sprocket turns a rotating prism immediately under the film gate. Light shines through the film to the prism and the picture is then back-projected on a ground glass screen. The lamphouse can be raised and lowered by hand to give direct access to the film in the picture gate. When the lamphouse is raised the lamp cuts out. You can then mark the film at the point at which you want to cut, lower the lamphouse again when the lamp will turn itself on again. If you are thinking of buying a machine of this kind make sure you get one which gives a clear bright picture. If it is dim and difficult to see you will soon find that you get tired of looking at it. Make sure too, that the film is easy to mark without having to burn your fingers on a lamp or turn the machine on its side. These are small points, but they are important enough when you are working on a machine for a long time.

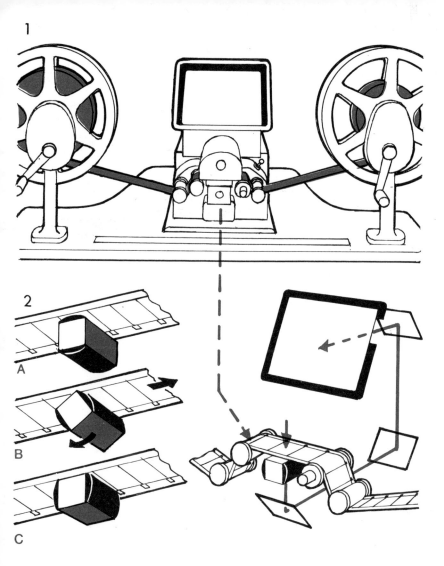

ANIMATED VIEWERS

For locating and assembling material

1. Layout

Viewers are normally fixed to a baseboard with rewind arms on either side. Picture is back projected via a rotating prism on to a small screen. The lamphouse, above the film can be raised and lowered so that you can mark your cutting point.

2. Projection by prism

A prism under the film path rotates, conducting the film images frame by frame via mirrors to the screen.

33

Sundry Cutting Room Equipment

Film bins or barrels are large metal or fibre bins lined with linen bags. Above the bins are editing racks, consisting of clips or pegs from which individual shots can be suspended. You need the trims bin when you start to break your rushes down into individual shots. You can hang each shot on a separate clip in the bin. When you make your first assembly you can take the shots out of the bin and assemble them in a roll. When you make your fine cut you can return the part of the scene you have not used to the appropriate peg in the bin, hence the name trims bin.

Wall cuts racks

Wall cuts racks are also found in many cutting rooms. They are basically the same as the trims bin except that they are designed, as the name suggests, to be permanently fixed to a wall, whereas trim bins are frequently mounted on wheels so that they can be moved if necessary.

Rewind arms

Different types of rewind arm are used in the cutting room. Hand powered rewinds need to be carefully chosen. Make sure they are well designed and ruggedly built and that the gear ratio is acting in your favour. Some rewinds are geared in a way that makes the simplest job a major effort. One turn of the handle to four turns of the spindle is the minimum to settle for. On the right of the editing bench you will need a rewind arm with a long spindle. It should be long enough to take four or five reels at a time. The reels can be placed on the same spindle alongside each other, separated only by small springs and, together, held firmly in position by a suitable clamp. Film fed through the synchroniser can be taken up on these reels and, by turning the rewind arm the tension can be taken up and the film wound on the reels. On the left of the synchroniser, at the left hand end of the work bench, a similar long spindle rewind arm can be fitted. Alternatively, a film horse can be used to hold the reels of film needed to supply the synchroniser.

Film horse

Film horses usually consist of three or four thin but sturdy metal poles about eighteen inches high and half an inch thick, permanently attached to a weighted metal base. A removable rod passes through the divisions of the partitions mid-way between the top of the poles and the weighted base. The film horse is designed to hold several reels of film side by side at the same level. Separate reels are placed in between the metal poles on the crossbar which passes through the centre of each reel. Film rotates when drawn off the reels and, as there is no obstruction, leaves the horse quite freely.

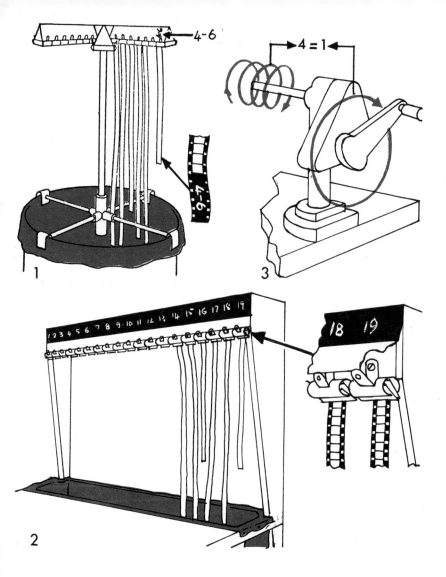

TRIMS BINS AND REWIND ARMS

1. A trims bin (film barrel in the USA)
Mark scene and take numbers, writing in chinagraph on and above the film before you hang shots in the bin. A linen bag limits scratching.

2. Wall cuts rack
Always mark the scene and take on the film as well as above the peg. If it falls off the peg it remains identifiable.

3. Rewind arm
Make sure it is geared in your favour. One turn of the handle to four of the spindle is the minimum to settle for.

Cutting Room Accessories

Besides the main items of cutting equipment some smaller tools are also needed. First of all you will want to mark the film at that point where you wish to make your cut. Grease pencils which write easily on film, are available in a number of different colours. White or yellow are best for marking picture—I personally prefer yellow because it is very easy to see. It can also be used to mark the back of magnetic sound-tracks, though black and red are also quite useful for this purpose. When you come to break down the rushes you may find that some scenes are too long to hang in a bin. They should be coiled on a plastic core and held in place with an elastic band, so a box of these should be handy. A felt tip pen is also very useful for writing on spacing. Obviously you will need joining tape. You will also use camera tape: a cloth tape which is sticky on one side, but can be peeled off fairly easily without causing damage to surfaces. Strips of camera tape are useful for attaching ends of film to reels and the tape is also widely used for bundling up piles of cans. A magnetic erasing pencil can also be useful. You can demagnetise small areas of magnetic soundtrack and can sometimes use it to delete either a syllable or part of a word. The active area of the tip of the pencil is a quarter of an inch. An adequate supply of can labels is also important. Always label every can with the title of the production and the name of the production company as well as giving details of what is in the can to avoid loss.

Split spools and film cores
In a cutting room film is not normally handled on reels with fixed sides. It is wound on small plastic cores. Though these cores will fit most editing machines they cannot be used on their own on upright rewind arms. They must be used to form the centre of a split reel — a reel with detachable sides. Film on cores can be laid on one side of a split reel. The other side can be laid on top of it and the two metal parts locked together with the core in between. The job takes a matter of seconds and enables cores with the split spool sides to be used with ease on projectors and rewind arms and elsewhere. Alternatively, a single flange plate can be attached to rewind arms. Plastic cores fit on the flange plates. It pays to be careful when handling film on cores. Be prepared for a loose wind, and make sure you do not let the centre of the reel drop out. Check the tightness of the wind before taking the film off the flange plates or before taking split spools apart.

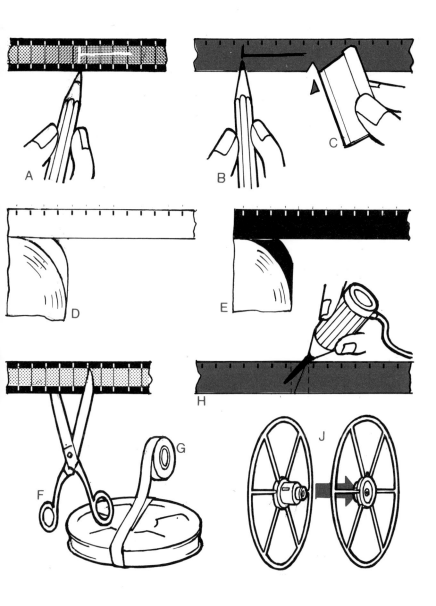

CUTTING ROOM ACCESSORIES

Chinagraph wax pencils will write on film (A) and on the shiny side of magnetic (B). De-magnetised razor blades (C), white spacing (D), black spacing (E) and a magnetic erasing pencil (H) for removing unwanted join clicks, are all essential. Brass (non magnetic) scissors (F), camera tape to tie cans together (G) and a split spool on which to hold film wound on cores (J) are all standard cutting room equipment.

37

Planning Picture Sequences

Films are made from sequences and sequences are made from shots. A sequence is rather like a paragraph in a book. It deals with a particular subject and is more or less complete in itself. A single shot is more like a single sentence. In a book, sentences are planned to go together in paragraphs. In a film shots must be planned in such a way that they can be assembled in sequences. Each shot must be planned so that it can be cut onto the shots which precede and follow it.

Definitions

Individual film shots are often referred to in the cutting rooms as scenes. This use of the word scene is really only correct in the case of a long take when the camera shoots an entire action sequence in one take. Strictly speaking, a scene really comprises a series of conjoined individual shots filmed from different camera viewpoints. However, in practice, the terms 'scene' and 'shot' are often loosely used. In a cutting room you may hear an editor ask his assistant to find Scene 10 Take 2. The meaning in this instance is that the editor wants his assistant to find one individual shot. You may also hear a director discussing the overall effect of the scene — for example 'did you think the scene in the cafe went well?' The director in this instance is probably referring to a number of shots all taking place in a cafe setting. So, the term is loosely used. In these pages I shall use the term shot.

Camera viewpoint

Most scenes can be observed from at least five different camera positions. For example, a man walking along a street can be seen from far away. In camera terms that means a long shot (L.S.). Here we see the whole street and the man is relatively unimportant. Going closer, to a medium long shot (M.L.S.) he becomes a little more important. Closer still, in a medium, or mid shot (M.S.) makes him even more prominent. In a close up (C.U.) we see only his head and shoulders and in a big close up (B.C.U.) we only see his face. Of course, the five camera positions mentioned do not all have to be used for each and every shot. Where the same subject has to be observed for some time, a change of viewpoint will be needed. Now you are going to have to cut those shots together, so, when they are filmed, your cutting requirements must be remembered. For example, in the case of the man walking down the street, the director must make sure that the man looks the same way in the mid shot and the close up. He must not be allowed to look down in one shot and ahead in the other. If he does, the two cannot be cut together satisfactorily.

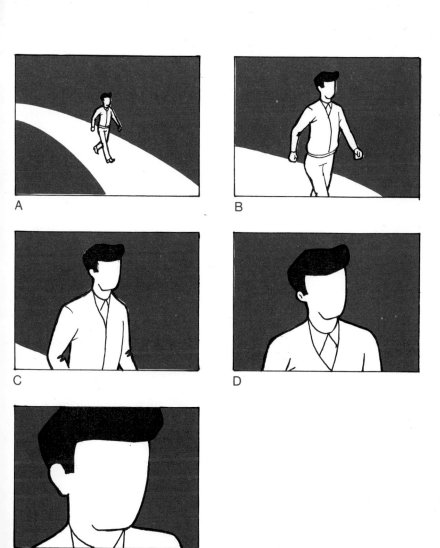

A   B

C   D

E

PICTURE REQUIREMENTS FOR CUTTING

Choice of camera angle
(A) Long shot. (B) Medium long shot. (C) Medium shot. (D) Close up. (E) Big close up.

Identifying and Printing Takes

As you probably will not see the filming taking place, you will have to rely on notes provided by the production team. Whenever film is shot detailed camera report sheets must be prepared by the camera assistant. The sheets serve a dual purpose. They contain instructions for the processing laboratory and they tell the editor what the day's film consists of. Camera report sheet forms may differ slightly in layout but the main facts they contain must always be the same.

Printing selected takes

One copy of the camera sheet is sent to the laboratory with the film. Another copy is sent to you in the cutting room. When you look at it you will note that many shots have probably been photographed a number of times. For example, for Slate 21 there may be take one, take two, take three and so on. Somewhere on the camera sheet you may find a note instructing the laboratory to 'print only circled takes'. What does this mean? All the original film exposed in the camera must be developed, but it may not all need to be printed. If, for example, a four hundred foot reel of 16mm film contains only three takes of a shot and only one is known to be good, it may be possible to print only the good take. The laboratory must be told which take to print and the normal way to do this is to encircle the scene and take number required on the camera sheet. On some camera sheets the letter 'P' for print is used instead of a circle to indicate the appropriate take. For example, on the camera sheet illustrated, Slate 21 has been shot three times. The Director has instructed the cameraman to print only take three. Slate 9, has also been shot three times but on this occasion both takes two and three are to be printed. Printing parts of reels like this is known as printing selected takes. It is a way of reducing costs.

False economies

It is only practicable to print part of a reel when each of the shots concerned is clearly identified on the head or the end. The best way to identify shots and takes is to use a clapper board. We'll hear more about that on page 120. It is not worth wasting laboratory time or risking extra handling of the camera original by ordering prints of parts of a reel containing no kind of shot to shot identification. Print the whole reel. There is no sensible alternative.

PICTURE NEGATIVE REPORT

Production Co **SOREL INTERNATIONAL**		Cameraman **JOHN CLARK.**	
Title **PETER USTINOU**		Date **25-3-73**	
Studio or Location **SINEKITTA**			

Order to	Laboratory	Stock & Code	Emulsion No.
KAYS		**7.254**	**653.14.1.**

Laboratory Instructions :— **EXT. DAY. NORMAL.**
**B/W C/L OF CIRCLED TAKES. NEG AND PRINT
TO SOREL INTERNATIONAL CUTTING ROOMS.**

Mag.	Length Loaded	Slate	Take	Counter Reading	Details
1	400	19	①	80	HOUSE EXT/C/A.
		20	①	400	CAR
2	400	21	1	10	N.G
		21	2	200	N.G
		21	③	315	OUT OF AIRCRAFT
		47	1	225	
		47	②	400	
3	400	2	①	60	
		9	1	120	
		9	②	240	
		9	③	390	

Total Loaded **1200'**	Total Printed **1825**	Total N.G. **655**

PRINT ALL CIRCLED TAKES

Signed : **R. Slater.**

CAMERA REPORTS

Camera report sheets differ in layout but always record the progress of
filming and provide instructions for processing the original and for making a
cutting copy. Note the takes which are not being printed.

You will need details of sound recorded during filming.

Identifying Sound Takes

If sound has been recorded while the film was being shot you will also need detailed sound report sheets. Like camera sheets, the layout of the sound report sheets may vary slightly from studio to studio but the key information they contain should always be the same. Sound report sheets should list the following:—

1. The name of the production and the production company.
2. The name of the recordist.
3. The sound recording studio responsible for re-recording the original sound to make a copy for editing purposes.
4. The tape speed and the type of recording equipment used.
5. Instructions for transferring the sound to perforated magnetic film, ready for cutting.

Using information provided

The sheet must also give as much information as possible about the various shots and takes. When a reel of picture film is processed not all the takes it contains need to be printed and, with master sound recordings, the same is true. Provided that shots and takes are clearly identified on the head or end, only selected takes need be copied, for editing. The sound report sheet will tell you which sounds have been transferred, and will give details of the footage at which each take begins and ends. We will see how the copy is made later but do not waste time looking for shots and takes which have not been copied. Study the sound sheet before you listen to the sound recording. You will save time and work. Having studied the sheets you will know what to expect. The sound should have its own aural identification on the beginning or the end of each take. You will have to play the tracks to hear the identification and you can use either a synchroniser, with a magnetic sound head, or a motorised editing machine. The sound and camera sheets will tell you how long each shot and take is in terms of film footage and that will make the process of identification even easier. Detailed sound and camera report sheets save time in a cutting room.

MAGNETIC SOUND REPORT   Nº 5191

Production "MOTORWAY"

Production Co SOREL FILMS		Mixer DAVID JONES	
Channel ELLAIR/NAGRA IV		Speed .7½ IPS	
Transfer to 16%. CENTRE MAG		Roll Nº 3	

Location SERVICE STATION — HESTON

Special Transfer Instructions :— 25 FPS. NAGRA IV.

50 CYCLE PULSE 7½ IPS.

Slate Nº	Take	Mark 'T' for Transfer	Remarks
17	1		SUPT. JOHNSON INTRO NS
17	2		NS
17	3		NS
17	4	T	POSSIBLE DOG BARK
17	5	N.S	
17	6	T	
W/T 17		T	ATMOS
23	1	T	
24	1		N.S
24	2	T	
7	1	T	
9	1		AIRCRAFT
9	2	T	

TRANSFER ONLY TAKES MARKED 'T'

SOUND REPORT SHEETS

Sheets must identify the type of recording system used and list each scene
and take. Note that *not* all the takes are being transferred to perforated
magnetic film. Sound sheets, like camera sheets, are available in many
different forms. The basic information shown here will be found on most
sheets.

The Film in the Camera

Sound and camera report sheets tell you what the reels of film you are going to cut consist of. The camera sheet also tells you what kind of film the picture has been photographed on. The type of film stock will be noted in the laboratory processing instructions.

Processing originals
You will find you deal with laboratories frequently in the course of cutting a film. The labs will be involved at many stages from the processing of the camera original to making prints of the final edited film. Camera originals are normally processed in a series of long tanks. The film runs through the tanks at a precise speed and the temperature of the chemicals in the tanks is very accurately controlled. A fractional variation can effect the colour balance of the film or the exposure. Extended (forced) development can compensate for inadequate exposure though it can also lead to an increase in grain size and a deterioration of picture quality. Modern negative developing machines run continuously at speeds of around 70ft of film per minute. In the case of 16mm colour negative original the time needed to pass from one end of the processing plant to the other is around one hour. A copy can then be made for editing.

You must know what type of film has been used in the camera. Though you will cut a copy made from the camera original you must know what the original film is. You may be editing a black and white copy. You must know if the original is in colour or black and white and you must know if the film has been shot on negative or reversal stock. How do the types differ?

Reversal and negative films
Reversal film when processed immediately produces a positive image in which the tones of the original scene are reproduced as they appear. On negative stock those tones are reversed. To get back to the original state the negative must be printed on a reel of positive stock. This operation will again reverse the polarity of the tones, returning them to their original form. If negative film is used in the camera, a cutting copy will be produced by making a rush print of the negative camera original on positive stock. If reversal film has been used in the camera, the processed reversal original can be rush printed on another reel of reversal stock.

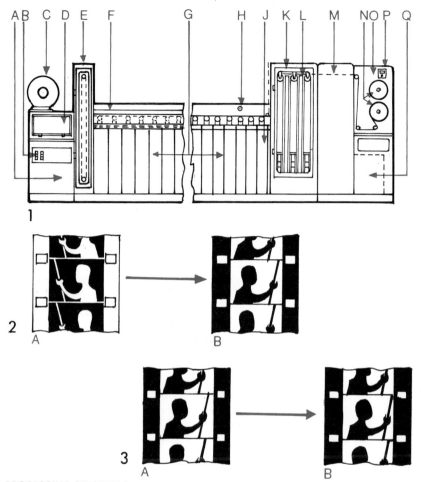

PROCESSING ORIGINALS

1. Typical daylight developing machine

(A) Solution/pump and valve housing. (B) Flowmeters. (C) Enclosed film magazine. (D) Stapling department for attaching new rolls. (E) Film reservoir. (F) Daylight cover for first section. Open tanks. (G) are used after the first stage. (H) A contact thermometer is fitted. (J) Final wash tank. (K) Drying cabinet. (L) Ducting for air jets. (M) Humidity Control. (N) Film Take Up. (O) Take Up Housing. (P) Automatic temperature control. (Q) Blower & main drive housing.

2. Neg/pos system

When a negative camera original is processed (2A) the tones of the original scene are reversed. By printing the negative on positive stock (2B) they can be returned to their original form.

3. Reversal system

When a reversal original (3A) is processed it immediately produces a positive image in which the tones of the original scene are realistically reproduced. Further positive copies can be made by printing the reversal originals on reversal stock (3B).

Copying the Original

In making a cutting copy the laboratory will use a motion picture printer. It is rather like a camera. It takes two reels of film — the processed camera original on one side and on the other a reel of new unexposed stock. The two reels pass through the machine together at speed. At one point, light is allowed to pass through the original film on to the reel of new stock. The original is thus re-exposed (printed) on the new stock. When the film has run right through, the original can be rewound and returned to its can and the new copy can itself be processed.

Grading
When making rush prints, laboratories tend to use the minimum number of exposure adjustments and colour corrections. Now when show prints of the final edited version of the film are made the laboratory will grade the edited original and assess the printing exposure and the colour correction needed for each shot. Grading (or "timing" in the U.S.A.) involves the assessment of the correct printer light and colour correction filters for each individual shot. When film is exposed in a camera the cameraman selects the most suitable exposure (lens aperture and filter) for everything he wishes to shoot. In the course of making a copy of an original film, the laboratory also make an exposure. The original negative is exposed on a reel of new stock in the film printer. The laboratory technician can adjust this exposure, according to how much light is allowed to pass through the original film on to the copy. When printing colour film, the grader also has to choose filters to balance the colours from shot to shot. This is highly skilled work. Today, a closed circuit colour television analyser is often used to provide a quick way of determining shot to shot grading values. But only show prints are corrected shot for shot.

Cinex strips
Rush prints are frequently made 'at one light'. They may sometimes be accompanied by a short strip of film known as cinex. Cinexes are widely used in 35mm filming. For 16mm work they are not so widely used but they can still serve a useful purpose. Cinex strips consist of a series of individual frames, printed at a range of exposures as a test. In the case of a black and white film, each frame of the strip to be printed at a different printer light, increasing from very light to very dark. In the case of a colour original, the density gradation will be replaced by a gradation of colour filter selections.

46

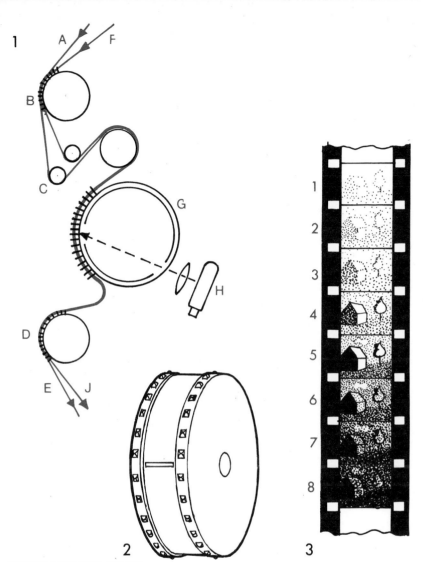

PRINTING CUTTING COPIES

1. Continuous contact printer

Film from an unexposed reel of positive stock (A) meets the processed original (F) at feed sprocket (B). The two pieces of film then pass round tension rollers (C) to the main sprocket (G) where the new stock is exposed in contact with the original by lamp and optical system (H). Finally, take up sprocket (D) moves the film on to separate take up reels for the original (J) and the newly exposed copy (E) which can now be developed.

2. Sprocket drum of continuous contact printer

The exposure aperture is formed in a fixed shell between rotating sprocket discs.

3. Cinex strip

Each frame of the test strip is printed at a different printer light increasing from very light (1) to very dense (8). Colour cinexes provide a gradation of colour filter selections instead of density gradation.

Cutting Copies

Cutting copies can be produced from every type of 16mm original film. The factors governing which material is to be used for printing are mainly economic.

Cutting copies of 16mm colour films
With 16mm originals, if the film which you are cutting has been shot in colour it will have been shot on either negative or reversal film. The most widely used 16mm colour negative is Eastmancolor and the most widely used 16mm colour reversal is probably Ektachrome. Both can be printed in colour or in black and white. Colour cutting copies are obviously more pleasant to work with. For some subjects they are essential. Black and white prints however, are considerably cheaper and are thus widely used. You can, of course, compromise by printing some reels in colour and some in black and white. Colour negative films (like Eastmancolor) can be printed on colour positive stock or on black and white positive stock.

Copies on panchromatic stock
When printing colour camera originals in black and white it is best to ask the laboratory to make the print on panchromatic stock. Pan stocks are sensitive to all the colours of the spectrum and will thus show up any edge fogging which could get lost on other black and white printing stocks. Colour reversal originals (like Ektachrome) can be printed either on colour reversal stocks or on black and white reversal. Again, the advice about Panchromatic stocks for black and white copies holds good. You may find that your laboratory charges more to produce a print on pan stock but it is well worth the small additional expense.

Black and white 16mm films
Black and white negative camera originals can be printed on black and white positive stock and black and white reversal camera originals can be printed on black and white reversal stock. Never project camera originals. Handle them with great care at all times. Always wear clean lintless gloves and make sure that the equipment you are using to handle the film is kept scrupulously clean. There is no safe way of projecting an original. If you have to examine it, use a rewind or synchroniser. Remember, if you scratch the original the damage will be there for ever. It will be reproduced on every copy of your film. I personally prefer to leave the camera original in the hands of the laboratory until the cutting copy is ready for neg cutting.

1

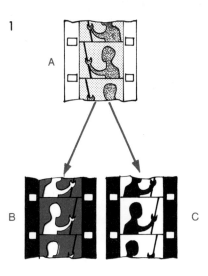

2

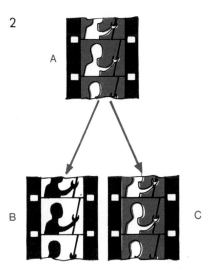

COPYING 16mm COLOUR ORIGINALS

1. Colour negatives
Colour negatives (like Eastmancolor) (A) can be printed on either positive (B)
or black and white positive (C). Check the edge numbers before you cut.

2. Reversal colour originals
Reversal colour originals (A) can be printed on either black and white
reversal stock (B) or on colour reversal stock (C).

49

Edge Numbers and Film Footage

The laboratory produce a copy of the original for you to cut. Except in the case of rush television news filming, the original film exposed in the camera should never be used for cutting. It is too valuable.

Final stage of cutting
When you have finished the job and the edited version is perfected, you can match the original to the cutting copy. This is done by matching sets of numbers on the side of the cutting copy with identical numbers on the edge of the original film. The numbers are matched and, where the cutting copy has been cut, the original is cut too. When the two match exactly the original can be printed on a roll of new, unjoined stock, thus making a copy of the edited version free of dirt, wear and scratches.

Edge numbers
The numbers on the side of the film are known as edge numbers (or key numbers). When you receive the rushes from the laboratory the numbers are the first things to check. Check before you start cutting. The numbers are on the camera original but you must make sure that the laboratory has copied them on the print. It is quite possible to mask off edge numbers in a laboratory printing machine. So, check and make sure that they are present before you start work. The neg cutter will rely on those numbers to match the original to your cutting copy but if they are not there he will have difficulty matching your work print. The work will take longer and it will be much more expensive. If the numbers are not printed through on the copy, return the copy and the original, if you have it, to the laboratory and ask them to print edge numbers on both.

Film footage
Film is measured in feet. A foot of 16m. film consists of 40 individual frames separated by perforations. Edge numbers normally occur once in every foot, though on some recently introduced film stocks they are to be found once every 20 frames. The numbers are always different. If you look at a piece of 16mm film the edge numbers might be, say, JH125833. If you now look forty (or occasionally at may be 20) frames further on you will find another number one digit higher: JH125834. Forty (or 20) frames back in the other direction there will be another number one digit lower. When rushes arrive in a cutting room you must log the numbers of the rushes before they are cut or broken down.

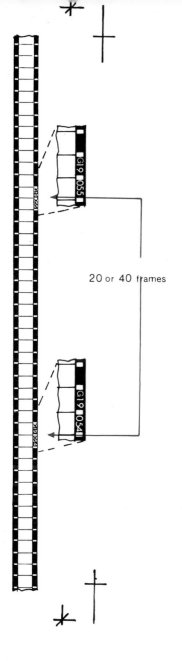

20 or 40 frames

EDGE NUMBERS AND FILM FOOTAGE

Also known as key numbers and footage numbers, edge numbers are incorporated in the film during manufacture. The numbers appear when an original is processed. On 16mm film there is normally one number every 40 frames or on some stocks one every 20 frames. On 35mm film there is one edge number every 16 frames.

Locating Scenes and Takes

Before you start to cut you should log the film you receive from the laboratory. Logging involves making a note of the edge numbers of each shot and take. This may sound a time consuming process. In fact it can save time for, while the reels are complete, logging is a simple process. Finding original material for an individual shot at a later stage of cutting can take time if there are no logging records to refer to. The log sheets provide a quick and easy way of locating a piece of original film.

Logging rushes

This job is best done on a synchroniser. You do not need the original material. Use the rush print. Unlock the synchroniser and put the film in the track nearest to you. Wind through the blank film on the head of the reel until you come to the first edge number. Make a note of the number and of the shot and take. If there is no clapper board to identify the shot number at the start, check the end of the take. If the film has been shot without visual identification, note a brief description of what the shot shows. On your log sheet note the edge number at the start of the shot. Zero the footage counter on the synchroniser and then wind on. Wind down to the first camera stop, the end of the first shot, and again note the edge number and the footage. You now have a record of what the first shot shows, the edge number at which it starts and the one at which it ends and you can tell immediately from your log sheets how long it runs. Note the number at the start of the next scene and repeat the process through to the end of the roll.

Minimising paperwork

Film students are sometimes taught to log not only the edge numbers, shot and take identification and film footages but also shot running time and the direction of the action portrayed. This may be a useful exercise but when you are involved with actually cutting a film you will probably find you do not have time for anything not essential. Logging edge numbers and shots and takes is essential. Making a note of the direction of the action in the shots in my opinion is not, and the running time of any shot can easily be worked out by calculating the edge numbers. You can certainly spend a lot of time adding details in paper work. You will probably prefer to get on with the job.

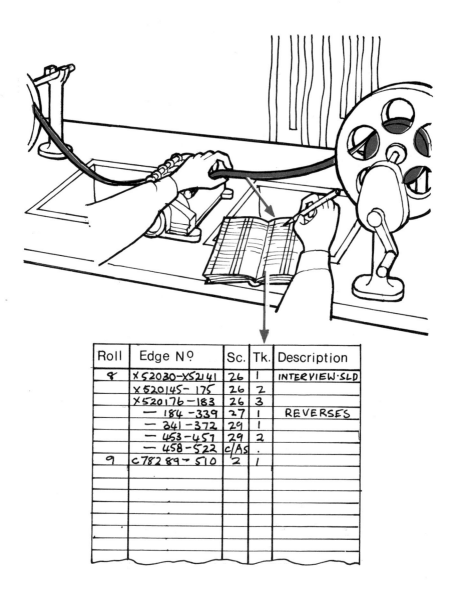

Roll	Edge N⁰	Sc.	Tk.	Description
8	X52030–X52141	26	I	INTERVIEW·SLD
	X520145– 175	26	2	
	X520176–183	26	3	
	— 184 –339	27	I	REVERSES
	— 341–372	29	I	
	— 453–457	29	2	
	— 458–522	c/As	.	
9	C78289–510	2	I	

LOGGING RUSHES

Noting scenes and takes

Wind through scene by scene noting the edge numbers at the start and end
of each scene and take. A detailed log enables you to trace the original of
shots needed for opticals or for reprinting, without having to wind through
every roll whenver you need a shot.

Breaking Down Rushes

You now have an exact note of what the reels of picture rushes contain. You also have the camera sheets to guide you, and a script or an assembly order from the film director. Now you can start to cut.

Separating scenes and takes

The first thing to do is to break down the rushes into individual scenes. Very few films are shot in the order in which the shots occur in the finished film and film shots are frequently photographed many times. Shots are often re-taken for artistic reasons. The director may not be happy with the way a scene has been played or with the action. Sometimes there are technical problems. The cameraman may make a mistake or aircraft passing overhead or other extraneous sounds may spoil a sound recording. So, you will find your rushes contain far more material than you will ever use. A cutting ratio of 5:1 is generally considered to be good. Of 500 ft of original camera material around 100 ft would be used in the final version. Cutting ratios vary enormously, depending on the subject and the people involved in photographing and directing the scenes. Some television production companies shoot a phenominal footage and you may find you have a very short time to cut a great deal of film. So, again, you will need to concentrate on essentials. The first essential is to break the rushes down.

Identifying the takes

Again, you can use a synchroniser. Wind through the roll and take out the shots and takes you intend to use. The director will tell you which takes he wants to use, the script will show the order in which they must occur. So, first of all, extract the shots you intend to use. Cut each individual shot out of the rolls of rushes and mark the shot and take number on the head of the scene using a chinagraph pencil and writing on the shiny side of the film. This shiny side is the base side of the film. All 16mm film consists of a cellulose base coated with emulsion. You should write on the base side — using a wax pencil. When you have written the scene and take number, cut the shot out of the roll and hang it in a trims bin (film barrel). You can then wind down to the next shot and repeat the process until you have all the shots you require hanging in the bin. If a shot is very long, it may perhaps be best coiled on an individual roll and held together with an elastic band. When the rushes have been broken down you can start to assemble them in script order and to do that you need to use a film joiner.

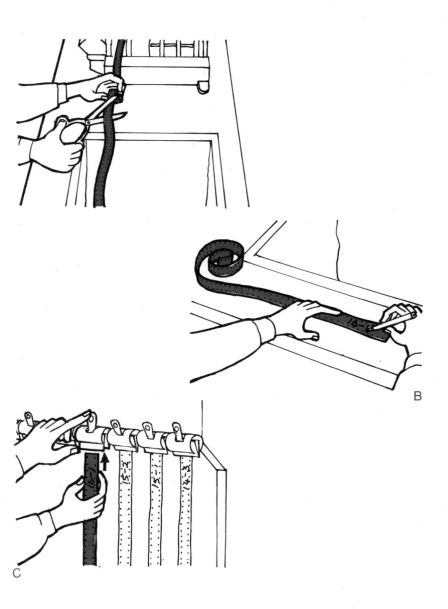

BREAKING DOWN RUSHES

Separate each scene and take (A) cutting on the blank frames. Write the scene and take number with a chinagraph pencil, writing on the cell (shiny) side of the film (B). Hang each shot on a peg in the trims bin or wall cut rack (C). You can also write the scene and take number above the clips if you wish. Long lengths can be wound in individual rolls held in place with an elastic band.

Joining with Tape

You will remember there are two main kinds of film joiner: one using film cement and the other for using tape. You will also recall that for cutting copy purposes a tape joiner is best. How do you make a join with a guillotine tape joiner?

Making the join

First you must mark the point at which you want to cut. You should do this by writing on the base side of the film with a grease pencil. Be precise. Mark the exact frame by drawing a line across the film opposite the perforations at which you want to cut and another line at right angles to it along the part of the shot you do not intend to use. The correct markings are shown on page 82. You can then move to the joiner. Raise the cutting blade and place the first of the pieces of film you want to join on the cutting block so that the point you have marked is immediately under the cutting blade. You can then bring the blade down and make your cut. Repeat this process with the other piece of film and then lay the two shots end to end so that they meet at the centre of the joiner block. Do not let them overlap. The two pieces should touch each other but not overlap. You can then draw tape across both strips of film, press the tape down and punch it clear of the film perforations. You do not need cement or patience, for the splice is completed in a second. Open the joiner up and take out your joined film, and return the trim to the trims bin.

When not to use tape

Tape joins are good for working purposes. They are strong and can be made quickly and easily. If you want to change a cut you simply peel a join and separate the two pieces of film. Joins made with tape can be used for picture and magnetic sound as we shall see later. But although they are ideal for cutting copy use, tape joins are not recommended for camera originals or for show prints because tape discolours with age and it can shrink or stretch. For original film repairs and for negative cutting cement splicers are essential.

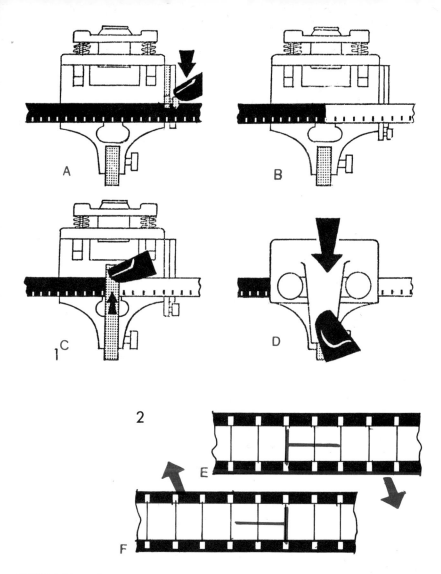

USING A TAPE JOINER

1. Tape joining stage by stage

(A) Place one piece of film across the joiner with the point at which you wish to cut on the right hand edge and bring down the knife to cut it. (B) Move the piece of film you wish to join to the centre of the joiner block and align so they are end-to-end but do not overlap. (C) Cover both pieces of film with tape. (D) Bring down the top of the joiner and press the handle to cut the tape and clear the perforations.

2. Indicating a cut

Indicate the point at which you wish to cut by drawing a line across the frame at the cutting point and another line at right angles to it, pointing along the part you want to lose. For example, in 2E the right hand portion is to be lost and in 2F the trim on the left.

Joining with Cement

When you join with tape the two pieces of film to be joined are laid end to end without an overlap. When a cement splice is made the two ends do overlap slightly. With the cement splicer the film is cut and emulsion is scraped off a small part of the edge of the end frame on one side of the join. Cement is applied to the clear film and the other piece of film to be joined is brought in contact with the cement-coated clear film before it has a chance to dry or harden. The second piece of film is not scraped clear of emulsion. If it were to be scraped clear the two pieces would allow light to pass straight through the film allowing a white flash to appear on the screen. The second piece of film is however cut to a slightly different length to allow a small part of the edge of the last frame to overlap the part of the other piece of film from which the emulsion has been scraped. The two pieces of film are therefore virtually welded together with film cement.

Film joins, or film splices as they are frequently called, should be made on the frame line between two pictures if they are to be imperceptible. When 35mm film is joined the frame line is so wide that the join can pass through unnoticed. On 16mm film the interframe area between pictures is much smaller so it is not possible to make an invisible splice. The normal method of avoiding a white flash as each join passes through is to neg cut and print the original film in checkerboard form, (See page 86). Cement joiners for 16mm usually produce a join which overlaps the frame line both ways. The edges of the join should go on the top of one frame and on the bottom of the other. A splice $\frac{1}{16}$in. wide is the narrowest practicable. A larger overlap will give added strength to a splice but will also appear more obvious when the film is projected.

Strong splice

Most cement joiners have a small, adjustable steel scraper blade. It is important to ensure that this is kept clean and free of emulsion build-up. Before joining valuable film, check the alignment of the blade by making a test splice with a piece of waste film.

Do not overdo the scraping. If you scrape off too much the splice will be weak. You can also weaken the splice by leaving it too long under pressure after applying the cement. To test the strength of a join you can lightly twist the two sides of the join in opposite directions. If the join is strong it will not part. Always use fresh cement.

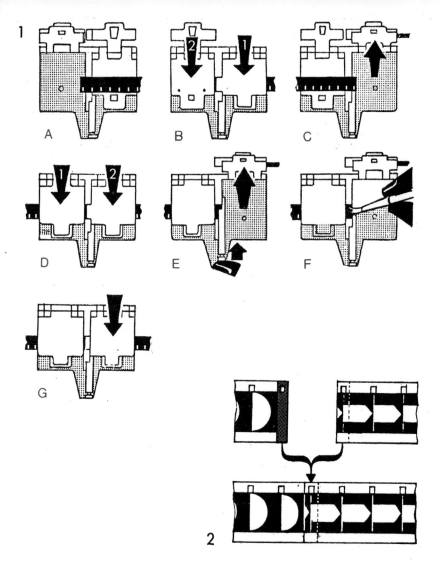

JOINING WITH CEMENT

1. Cement splicing stage by stage

(A) Place one piece of film on the right hand side of the splicer. (B) Lower the right hand side and bring the left hand side down to cut the film opposite. (C) Raise the right hand side again and insert film in the left. (D) Bring the right hand side down again to cut the film on the left. (E) Raise the right hand side and scrape the piece of left side film which is still visible. (F) Apply cement to the left hand portion. (G) Bring the right hand side down in contact with the wet cement. Wait about 10 seconds, release both sides and inspect.

2. Overlapping splice

When you join with cement the two pieces of film normally overlap. The size of the overlap can be reduced by joining on a special frame line joiner.

Film Leader

Now we can get on with the first assembly. At the start of your work print you will need a film leader. You will use two different kinds of leader in the course of cutting. Blank leader, consisting of a coated or uncoated base and academy leaders, containing a descending series of numbers, usually starting at eleven or ten and running in descending order down to three. There are then two feet of blank film before the point at which you should join the starter by the sound or picture. Blank leader film is frequently used for spacing and to protect the beginnings and ends of film. It is widely used when preparing separate sound tracks as we shall see later. Academy leaders are designed to go at the start of every reel of film. They serve a dual purpose. They ensure that there is always enough film to thread through a projector and they are long enough to ensure that the machine projecting the film is up to running speed before the first picture is reached. When films are being cut with separate magnetic tracks they also provide a common synchronism point for sound and picture.

There are several different types of leader. In Britain the BBC have their own standard leader. SMPTE Universal and SMPTE Television leaders, both named after the Society of Motion Picture and Television Engineers, are widely used. But perhaps the most common is the academy leader.

Academy leaders
The name of this leader is derived from the American Academy of Motion Picture Arts and Sciences which originated it. The synchronising section is normally opaque with the exception of numbered frames the first of which is marked "picture start" at a distance of 192 frames ahead of the first scene in the reel. In the academy leader these numbered frames occur at 16 frame intervals and run from 11 down to 3 after which all the frames are opaque up to the begininning of the picture. There is also an academy leader specially designed for television use. The synchronising numbers occur at intervals of 24 frames. For T.V. networks running at 24 frames per second this means, of course, that the numbers on the leader come up at 1 second intervals. The numbers start at 8 and run down to 2, instead of 11 to 3 on the standard academy film leader. Also, the opaque frames between the numbers have been changed on the television leader to a series of middle densities with a continuously moving wedge pattern rather like a clock, to denote the passing of each second. Academy television leaders have been designed to help T.V. cueing. They are particularly helpful when film inserts are being used in live T.V. programmes.

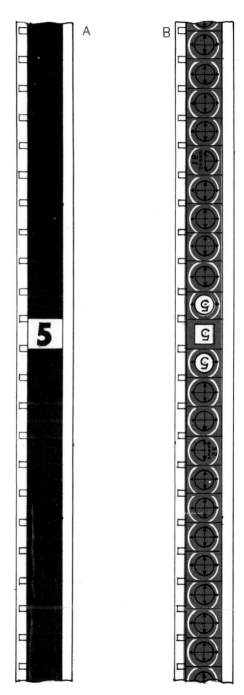

A

B

(A) Section of an Academy leader

"Picture Start" is 192 frames ahead of the first scene on the reel. Numbered frames occur at 16 frame intervals and run from 11 down to 3 after which the remaining 47 frames are opaque up to the start of the reel.

(B) Television leader

The arrow points on the mid-density frames on the television leader (B) indicates the limits of the scanned area of the frame. The synchronising numbers occur at intervals of 24 frames so for TV networks transmitting at 24 fps they appear at one-second intervals and thus make accurate telecine cueing easier.

Making a First Assembly

Start your first assembly with an academy leader. You should join some blank leader on the head of that, to provide additional protection. Mark on the head of the leader the title of the film and the reel number and the words "cutting copy action". You can make your first assembly on a motorised editing machine if you wish but a picture synchroniser is really just as suitable. Place an empty reel on the rewind arm on the right hand side of the synchroniser, wind your leader into it and then turn to the first scene in your film. You will find it hanging in the trims bin, or if it is a very long take, rolled on its own plastic core.

Backing tape joins
The main objective of the first assembly is to get scenes in script order not to cut them to length or for effect. The first assembly is never a technical masterpiece. So, ensure that you have the right scene to start with, cut off the clapper board identifying the head of the shot and join the head of the shot on to the leader with a tape join. You only need to tape one side of the join. It is sometimes a good idea to back all tape joins, by applying another piece of tape to the opposite side of the film before dubbing, but at first assembly stage it is not necessary to back joins. Indeed it can be a nuisance, because many of the cuts made in the first assembly will be changed when the fine cut is made and you will simply waste time peeling double backed joins. When you reach the end of the first shot, mark the point at which you intend to cut to the second. You can then find the second shot and join it on to the first and continue in the same way until the trims bin is empty and you have a complete roll of assembled shots.

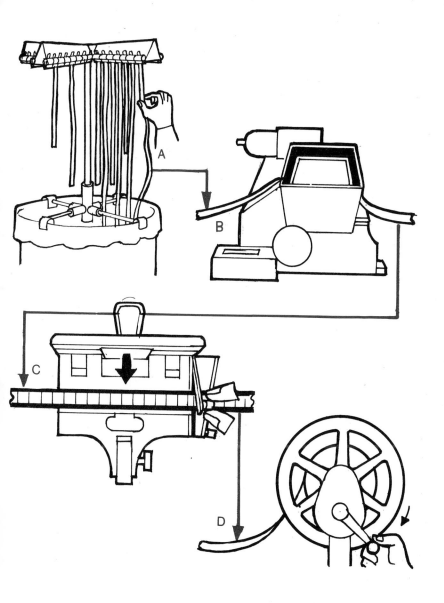

STARTING A FIRST ASSEMBLY

Putting shots in sequence

Take shots out of the trims bin (A). Using either a synchroniser or a viewer check the identity of the shot and pick your cutting point (B). Mark the cutting point and join with tape (C). Wind the assembled shots on reel (D) and return any trims to the trims bin identifying them with a wax pencil first.

Continuity Cutting

Where do you cut when making a first assembly? The cutting point in some shots will be made obvious by the need to avoid a repetition of the action — a double take. If, for example, you have to cut together two different shots both showing a man walking down a street you will find that you have to match the action when cutting from shot to shot. You have to note the pace at which the man is walking and the position of his feet at the point where you make your cut. If you mismatch the action the man will appear to take a skip. If you cut at exactly the same point out of one shot and into the other the action will be smooth and the cut will not disturb the continuity of the action. Making cuts like this is basically a matter of commonsense — of matching the action when cutting from shot to shot.

Choice of cutting point
Other cutting points will not be so definite. There will be several possible points at which to cut into or out of the shot. For example, if cutting from a shot of a train arriving at a station to a different shot of an aircraft taking off at an airport you can cut at almost any point. In the first assembly it is probably best to leave the shots full length. Then, when you know what commentary has to be laid over the shots or what music and sound effects are available you can trim the shots to length. It is always easier to cut them down afterwards rather than find trims and put them back.

Practical advantages of tape joins
With tape joins it is much easier to alter a cut. You simply peel off the tape and if you want to extend a shot you replace the trim, checking the edge numbers to make sure that you have not lost any frames unintentionally (see page 80). Now, if you were to join your assembly with cement, alterations would be far more difficult to make. When you make a cement join you automatically lose frames to provide the necessary overlap. Once those frames have been lost they can not be replaced and you would have to use frames of spacing in their place. So in that way tape joins are great time savers.

MATCHING CUTTING POINTS

Action cuts

When cutting two shots of the same subject together match the action at your cutting point. Make sure that the man's feet are at the same angle in the mid shot and the close up. Then, when the two shots are projected, the cut will appear smooth and satisfactory. If you pick the wrong point the man will appear to skip.

65

Cutting a Simple Sequence

You will often find that you have to cut together sequences where the same subject features in a number of consecutive shots. I have already suggested as an example two shots of a man walking down a street. Consider another example, and the choice of possible cutting points. The sequence might perhaps show a car arriving, the driver getting out and walking off. The scene may have been shot from three different positions. There may first be a long shot showing a section of the street with the car drawing up. Then there may be a medium shot concentrating attention on the man. This could be followed by a close-up, again featuring the man. Now, when you assemble these shots, where should you cut? Your aim should be to preserve the visual continuity of the scene and to avoid a double take. You can do this by matching the action at your cutting point.

Matching action cuts
In the long shot we see the car draw up and stop. The man gets out and walks away. In the close-up the car has already stopped and we just see the car door opening and the man getting out and walking away. Now, when you cut from the long shot to the medium shot you must avoid a repetition of the action — like the car door opening twice. Let the car stop in long shot then cut, before the car door opens to the medium shot. Alternatively, let him get out of the car in the long shot and cut to the medium shot later, carefully matching his position and actions so that they are precisely the same in the long shot and the medium shot at your cutting point. Make sure the man is doing the same thing in the same way at the same point. He must not be looking down in the long shot and ahead in the medium shot. Is his mouth closed and are his hands in the same position in both shots at your cutting point? Match the action here and when you cut from the medium shot to a close-up and you will preserve the continuity of the scene.

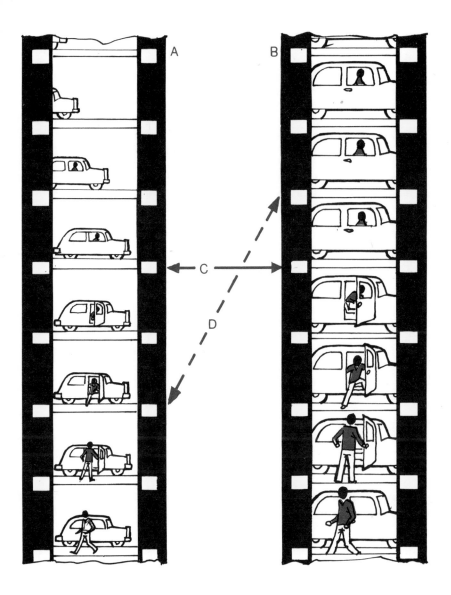

ASSEMBLING ACTION SEQUENCES

Avoid a double take

When cutting out of the long shot of the car arriving and stopping (A) into the close up (B) you must match the action at your cutting point. If you cut at (C) after the car has stopped but before the door has opened, the cut will work. If you cut at (D) you will have a double take, allowing the car door to open twice.

67

Avoiding Continuity Errors

You will sometimes find that two different shots of the same subject cannot be cut together satisfactorily even though they were planned to do so. This is often due to bad direction. There are other reasons too. Consider an example. The cameraman has filmed a footballer scoring a goal. He has concentrated on the man who scores the goal but, just after the ball entered the net, one of the spectators bumped into him and jogged his arm. The rushes show the results — a number of frames of cloud and sky filmed while the cameraman tried to regain his balance. It looks unprofessional and if you simply cut out the frames where the cameraman was jolted the continuity of the sequence will be disturbed. The man will be scoring his goal one moment then, without warning, running in the opposite direction. The cut would be ridiculous, so how do you solve the problem? You can solve it by using a cutaway.

Cutaways

A cutaway is a shot showing something other than the main theme of the action. It must, of course, be relevant. In the football example it must not show the scorer or the goal so a shot of spectators cheering would be ideal. When you cut, start with the shot of the goal being scored. Hold onto it, up to the point where the cameraman was jogged, and then insert the cutaway shot. Hold the cutaway for a few seconds then cut back to the scorer running back in triumph.

Jump cuts

If the cutaway were not used, and the two shots of the man scoring the goal and running back were cut together without an intermediate shot, the resulting cut would be what is known as a jump cut — a cut interrupting the normal sequence of the action. You can make a jump cut by removing a piece of film from a continuous sequence of action and joining the ends together. Moving objects will then be seen to jump instantly into new positions, hence the name jump cut. Unwanted jump cuts can be omitted by using cutaways but there are occasions when jump cuts are deliberately planned and used. If, for example, a number of shots of the same subject, filmed from different camera positions, are cut together quickly, as jump cuts, the effect can sometimes be quite interesting. But jump cuts should be an exception and not a rule. Your main aim should be to preserve smooth continuity. Jump cuts can be used where they serve a definite purpose but they must not be over used and should never be made accidentally.

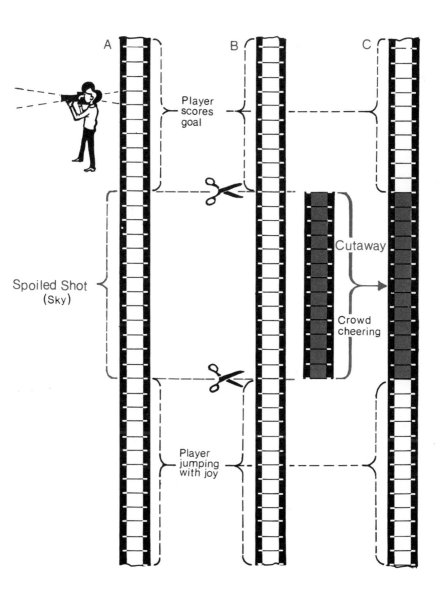

A

B

C

Player
scores
goal

Cutaway

Spoiled Shot
(Sky)

Crowd
cheering

Player
jumping
with joy

SOLVING CONTINUITY PROBLEMS

Cutaways

By using the cutaway of a cheering crowd in the edited cutting copy (C)
continuity rules are observed and a jump cut eliminated. To simply cut out
the spoiled shot in the neg (A) and in the cutting copy (B) without inserting a
cutaway would make the players appear to change position instantly as if by
magic. Cutaways must always be relevant. Make sure the crowd is cheering
and not looking glum or gazing in the wrong direction.

69

Optical Effects: Dissolves

There are several ways of moving from one shot to another besides cuts. In a dissolve (or mix as it is often called) one shot gradually merges with another until it replaces it. Another way of moving from shot to shot is to fade out one and fade in another. These effects, and others like them are known as optical effects. Only a cut can actually be made by you. All the other transitions have to be produced by a laboratory acting on detailed instructions supplied by you. How are optical effects prepared?

In a dissolve one scene merges with another and gradually replaces it. In essence it is a fade out and a fade in superimposed. The outgoing shot starts to fade out and, at exactly the same point, the incoming shot starts to fade in. Dissolves can be printed when show prints are produced if the camera original film is neg cut in A and B rolls (See page 92).

As the shots gradually merge, where do you join the two shots in your work print? You should join at the centre point of the planned dissolve. And, most important of all, always ensure that there is an adequate overlap available.

Optical overlaps

When the camera original is matched to the cutting copy the outgoing and incoming shots must be overlapped so that a fade out and fade in can be superimposed. So, when you make your cut, remember this overlap and ensure that there is enough film left on either side of your cutting point. Dissolves can be long or short. With practice you find you can visualise the length of dissolve you want but 12, 24 and 48 frame (overall) dissolves are most common.

The length you use depends on the effect you want to produce and on the amount of overlapping original film that is available. The overlap should be half as long as the total length of the optical effect. So, if you have a 48 frame dissolve, you will need 24 extra frames on each shot at each side of the centre point at which you make your cut in the work print. When you join the centre point in your cutting copy mark the whole of the dissolve with the symbol shown on page 91. When the original is matched to the cutting copy the negative cutter will then overlap the outgoing and incoming shots on the camera original (see diagram). When the laboratory prints the two rolls they will start to fade out roll A and fade in roll B at the same point.

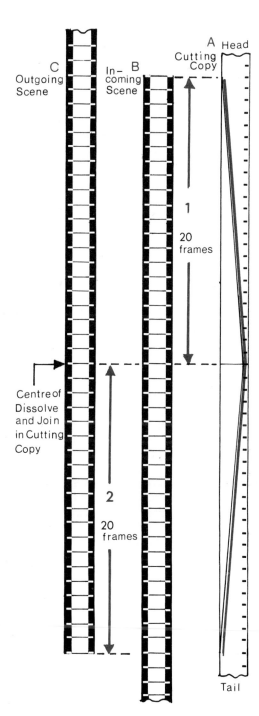

C
Outgoing
Scene

In–
coming
Scene

B

A Head
Cutting
Copy

1

20
frames

Centre of
Dissolve
and Join
in Cutting
Copy

2

20
frames

Remember the overlap
Join your cutting copy (A) at
the centre point of the
dissolve, checking first to
ensure that there is enough
overlap. This 40 frame
dissolve requires a 20 frame
overlap on the outgoing
scene (C) after the centre
point and on the incoming
scene (B) before it.

Tail

Single Roll Optical Effects

The preparation of opticals in the cutting copy of a film is not confined to cases where the camera original is to be neg cut in two separate rolls. Optical effects can still be produced where the film is to be neg cut in a single roll but as you cannot physically overlap the two components on the original film, you must make a single duplicate copy incorporating the optical effect which can then be cut into the edited roll of camera original.

Identifying an optical

The camera original is the master film. You start to make a cutting copy in the normal way and to edit a cutting print. If you want to dissolve from one sequence into another you mark the dissolve and cut it in the way already described, joining at the centre point of the optical effect. When you have done this you look at the edge of the film, and note the edge numbers on the two shots making the dissolve. These numbers must be used to guide the laboratories in making the single roll duplicate master incorporating the optical effect to be intercut with the camera original in a single roll. By using the numbers on the side of the film you can pinpoint the precise frame at which you wish the duplicate to start, the dissolve to begin and end and the duplicate to finish. When you have noted the numbers on the cutting copy the same scenes can be removed from the camera original. The laboratory can then make the dissolve for you and send you a single roll of duplicate master film incorporating the effect.

Quality of duplicate master materials

Duplicates are never of as good quality as originals and single roll duplicates incorporating optical effects are never as good as optical effects printed in the course of making copies from A and B rolls. Today most 16mm films are neg cut in two rolls but there may be occasions when a single roll is needed and you should therefore know how duplicate effects of this kind can be prepared. Duplicates (dupes) are always more grainy than originals, definition is poorer and the colour quality can also suffer. Camera original film is often referred to as the master and a duplicate of the original a dupe master. When the camera original is negative film the term dupe negative is frequently used or, if the film is in colour, internegative. Where the camera original has been filmed on reversal stock, duplicate master or duplicate colour master are the terms most widely used.

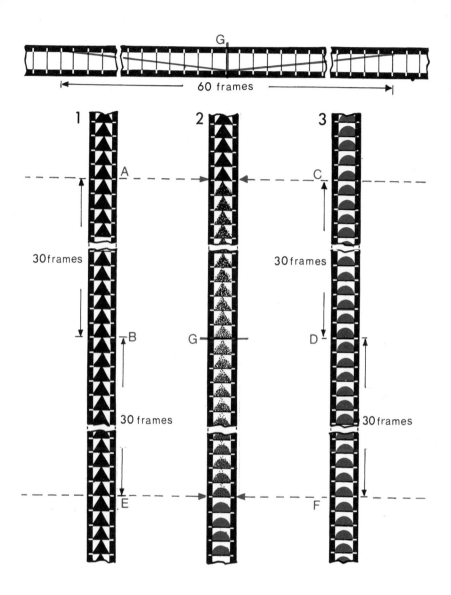

SINGLE ROLL DISSOLVES

Single roll dupe

A 60 frame dissolve has been joined in the cutting copy at the centre point (G). The outgoing scene (1) starts to fade out at (A) 30 frames before the centre point (B). At the same time the incoming scene (3) starts a 30 frame fade in (C). At 30 frames past the centre point the outgoing fade out ends (E) and the incoming shot is now fully faded up (F). On the single roll optical dupe (2) the fade in and fade out are visually superimposed, thus producing the dissolve effect.

Ordering Single Roll Optical Dupes

To order a single roll optical dupe first look at the cutting copy and note the edge numbers on the start of the outgoing shot on your dissolve. Always start the duplicate at the beginning of the shot. Dupe the whole shot, not just the part incorporating the dissolve. So, look at the centre of your dissolve and then go back to the start of the outgoing shot. Take the edge number nearest the join and make a note of the number on a pieces of paper. It may be NZ3245974 for example. Now you have pinpointed a number of frames, over which the number spreads. As you must be much more precise, locate one frame by putting a box round the number on which a particular series of figures occur. For example, if you put a box round the figures 74, you immediately designate one particular frame — the frame on which the figures 74 occur. Now you can be even more precise. You can indicate the exact frame at which you want the duplicate to start. When you put a box round the figures 74 you select one specific frame. Now if you look again at the piece of film you will find that on either side of the number you have listed, at one foot intervals, are two other numbers. One is NZ3245973 and the other is NZ3245975. From these numbers you can gauge the direction of the film. Now look at the frame you have specified with a box. Where, in relation to that frame, is that start of the shot? Is it to the right, or to the left? Is it nearer 3245973 or 3245975? Count the number of frames between the frame you have marked with a box and the frame at which the shot starts and write the number down. Now note the direction. Is it nearer the higher number than the one you first noted or nearer the lower one? if it is nearer the higher one put a plus sign next to the number of frames you have just noted. If it is in the opposite direction, mark a minus. You have now pinpointed the exact frame at which the shot starts.

Length of dupes
Now look at the start of the dissolve and repeat the process. Indicate the precise frame at which you want the dissolve to start by using the edge numbers. You can then repeat the process for the incoming shot using an edge number to indicate the point where you want the dissolve to end and another one to indicate the point at which you want the duplicate to end. Always duplicate the whole shot, never just the length of the optical effect. You will then make the laboratory grader's work much easier and make the whole shot of the same technical quality.

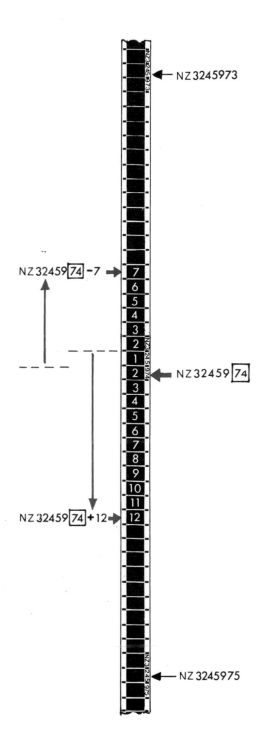

NZ 3245973

NZ 32459 74 -7

NZ 32459 74

NZ 32459 74 +12

NZ 3245975

**Edge number
identification**
By putting a box round
numbers falling on one frame
you can pinpoint a particular
frame. If there is no number
on the frame you want to
pinpoint, identify one frame
of the nearest number and count
the number of frames
between it and the frame you
want to pinpoint. If it is nearer
the higher number indicate
the number of frames
separating the two points by
using a plus sign—if it is
nearer the lower use a minus
sign.

75

Optical Effects: Fades and Freezes

When you want to fade in or fade out you must again mark your cutting copy indicating the effect you require. If you want a scene to fade in, mark an elongated letter V with the narrowest part at the start of the fade in and the wide part at the point where the picture is fully faded in. For a fade out simply reverse the symbol: the wide part starts where the fade out begins and, by the point where the two sides of the V meet, the picture will have faded out completely. You do not need to allow for an overlap with fades. The laboratory will simply cue their printing machines to fade in or fade out at the appropriate point. Again, the lengths of a fade are calculated in frames. Normally 8, 16, 24, 32 frames and so on.

Freeze Frames

You may sometimes want to hold one frame of a particular shot and repeat it without continuous movement. This is known as 'freezing frame' and it is an optical effect. The quality of freeze frame shots is often far from good. Grain is more pronounced and definition will suffer. It is, of course, essential to choose a frame free of blemishes. How do you order freeze frame dupes?

A freeze frame cannot be printed in the course of printing ordinary copies of a film. You have to arrange for duplicate master materials to be produced. So, if you want to freeze at a particular frame, first mark the frame on the cutting copy. Then look for the nearest edge number and pick one frame on which a definite part of the number appears. Perhaps the number is DZ47954. Make a note of the part of the number nearest the frame you want to freeze. If the figures 54 at the end of the edge number occupy one individual frame, count the number of frames between that frame and the frame you want to freeze. Then write the whole edge number on a sheet of paper putting a small box round the figures 54. You have now pinpointed one specific frame and you can count the number of frames betweeen that frame and the frame you want to freeze. Write that down on the paper too. In between the two numbers you must again write either a plus or a minus sign. If the frame you want to freeze is on the side of the number nearest the head of the roll (the lower edge number) put a minus sign. If it is on the opposite side — nearer the tail of the roll — put a plus sign. You have then pinpointed the exact frame you want to freeze.

1

HEAD

1.Marking fades

To make a fade out on your cutting copy (1) draw an elongated letter 'V' with the wide point starting where the fade out should start and the point where the two sides meet where it should end. For a fade in, reverse the process.

FADE OUT →

FADE IN →

TAIL

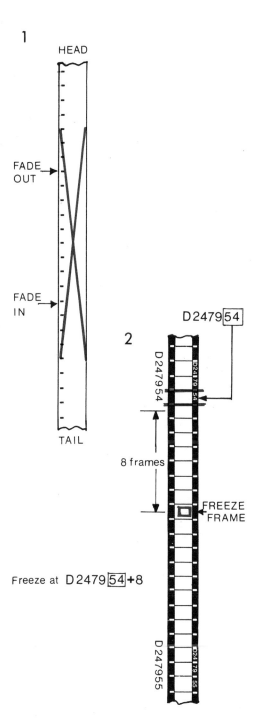

2

D 2479 54

D 247954

8 frames

← FREEZE FRAME

Freeze at D 2479 54 +8

D 247955

2. Pinpointing a freeze frame

By using edge numbers you can pinpoint the frame you want to freeze. Pick the nearest edge numbers; D 247954. Note that the figures 54 appear alone on one frame. Box those figures to identify that one frame. Now count the number of frames between it and the frames you want to freeze. You are moving towards the tail and towards higher numbers, so use a plus sign to point out that the freeze frame is eight frames further on—at D 247954+8.

77

Extending and Fine Cutting the Action

Stretch printing

You may sometimes find you want to slow down the action of a shot. That also involves using optical printing techniques. For example you might have some old film shot in the days of silent movies when filming speeds of around 16 frames per second prevailed. When projected at today's sound film speed of 24 or 25 frames per second the people appearing in the scenes appear to walk unnaturally fast. You can reduce the jerkiness of this effect by making a duplicate master which is "stretch printed". When a shot is stretch printed every second frame of original is printed twice. When the duplicate is shown at normal speed the original jerky movements are considerably smoothed out. The laboratories load an optical film printer with the old film and with new stock. The two pieces of film are run through the machine together and the old film is re-exposed frame by frame, normally exposing each shot twice, on the new roll of stock.

The exact number of exposures given for each frame will depend on the cranking rate of the camera making the exposures on the original film. You must decide on the rate you want the laboratory to use. Motorised editing machines can be time-calibrated to help you judge the treatment required. The rate I have indicated is the one normally used but if the camera was cranked at a very slow rate, three or more exposures per frame can be used. Again, when the duplicate master has been produced it should be printed to make a cutting copy.

Recutting the first assembly: (Fine Cut)

When the first assembly has been prepared you can start to re-cut it and make a finer cut. Having got the shots in the right order you will now want to cut them to length and for effect. The length of time you hold each shot can be used to emphasise a particular point or situation. By carefully picking your cutting points you can give each sequence a definite pace. There is plenty of scope for creative editing but much must be learnt in practice. It would, of course, be quite possible to make all the sequence of the film the same length but an audience would soon get bored with the result. The pace must be varied. If a scene is dramatic, you can make it more dramatic by shortening the lengths of the shots as the drama reaches its climax. If you wish to recreate a calm restful atmosphere you could use dissolves.

78

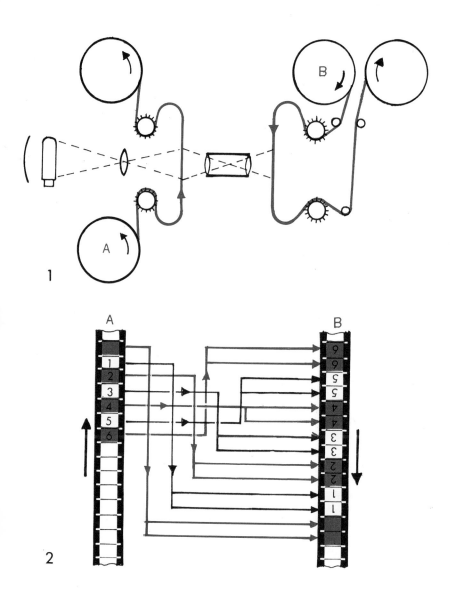

STRETCH PRINTING

Printing step by step

1. An optical printer enables an original (A) to be moved frame by frame while new stock used to make a duplicate (B) is advanced at a different speed. The exact number of exposures depends on the cranking rate of the original film. Often, each original scene (2A) is exposed twice when a stretch-printed duplicate (2B) is produced.

Changing and Patching Cutting Copies

In the course of perfecting your final edited version you will often find that you want to alter a cut. You may wish to extend a scene or to shorten it. This should not present any problem. Simply replace the trim of the scene you wish to extend, and make sure that no frames are missing. Then mark the rejoined section with an unintentional cut sign (illustrated opposite). How do you ensure there are no frames missing when you replace a section of a shot? Again, edge numbers provide a safety check. Often the action itself will give you a clue. If frames are missing the picture will jump. The safest way to check is to refer to the edge numbers on either side of the section you have replaced. Remember that there should be one edge number in every 40 frames (or every 20 frames on some 16mm stocks) so it is simply a question of counting the frames between the numbers on either side of the section you have replaced. By marking the cutting copy with the unintentional cut sign you will instruct the negative cutter to ignore the cut when the camera original is matched to the edited copy.

Repairing cutting copy damage

You may sometimes find that a section of the cutting copy gets 'chewed up' by some piece of editing machinery. In the ideal cutting room this sort of thing does not happen but in practice it happens quite often, so it is worth knowing what to do in the event of a section of a shot becoming unprojectable. You simply cut out the frames which are damaged and replace them to the same length with some spacing, again marking the unintentional cut sign on either side of the spacing section. If the damaged part of the film occurs at a point where you have already made a picture cut, you should mark the number of frames on either side of the cut and indicate the exact frame at which the cut is to be made on the spacing. The negative cutter will then be guided by your wax pencil marks. In Figure B white spacing has been used to replace a damaged section of one shot. The damaged section is in the middle of the shot so unintentional cut signs have been placed at both ends. In Figure C the damaged section is replacing the end of one shot and the start of another. The point at which the cut was made has been indicated and the arrows show the negative cutter exactly where to cut the camera original.

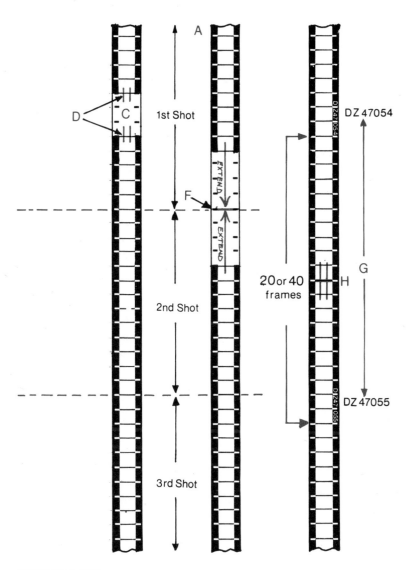

ALTERING A CUT

Using build up

At (D) build up has been used to replace lost or damaged frames. Note the 'unintentional cut' symbols at each end of the spacing. The neg cutter will ignore the cut, carrying the original scene through. In film (A) the damaged section includes a point where two shots have been cut together. The cutting point is marked with a wax pencil together with instructions to the neg cutter to extend the appropriate shots in each direction. In film (H) a cut has been altered. The trim has been found and replaced. The editor has checked the key number to ensure that no frames have been lost and has then marked 'unintentional cut'.

81

Augmenting Original Film

In the course of cutting your film you may sometimes have to use stock library shots. Sometimes the cost of shooting a scene may prove prohibitive, so a library stock has to be used instead. Perhaps the film you are cutting needs a few shots of the harbour at Hong Kong. The production budget is unlikely to allow for a camera crew to go out and shoot just a few establishing shots. So library stock material may have to be used instead. Some of the larger film production organisations have their own libraries of stock shots. If the film you are cutting is not being produced for a company with a library you will have to obtain stock shots from outside sources.

Ordering stock footage

First, contact the library and give them precise details of the scene you need. Tell them exactly what it must show giving as much detail as possible. It is quite useless saying that you want shots of Hong Kong. It is equally useless saying that you want shots of Hong Kong harbour. You must be much more precise. You must explain that you want a contemporary long shot giving a general view of the harbour on a fine day. Then you must give as much detail of what you expect to see in the scene. Tell the library the sort of film you are making and the type of film stock it has been shot on. They will then provide viewing copies of a number of shots which they think might be suitable. The viewing prints will give you an idea of the content of the shots and, when you have found the suitable take, you can ask the library to prepare a duplicate master to intercut with your camera original. They should also be asked to prepare a cutting print.

Libraries will never part with original film. If the library film was originally shot on 16mm Ektachrome, you should ask for a duplicate Ektachrome master to be produced, together with a print for editing purposes. If the film was shot on Eastmancolor they will provide a colour interpositive or a colour internegative. If the film is black and white they will make a fine grain duplicating positive and a black and white duplicate negative. Edge numbers on stock shots are frequently unclear. Before cutting anything, make sure the numbers are legible. If they are not, numbers should be printed in ink on the side of the duplicate master film and on the cutting copy.

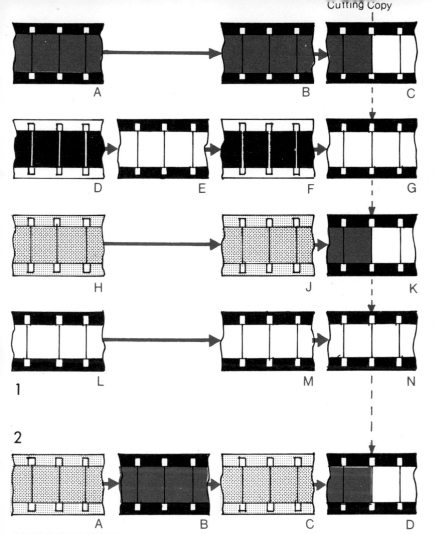

Cutting Copy

USING STOCK SHOTS

1. Duping library material

From Ektachrome originals (A) you can make an Ektachrome dupe (B) thence either a black and white or colour reversal cutting copy (C). Black and white neg originals (D) must first be printed on fine grain duping positive (E). The F.G. dupe pos can then be printed on black and white dupe neg stock (F) which can itself be printed on black and white pos (G) to make a cutting copy. Colour neg (H) can be directly printed on to 16mm colour reversal interneg (CRI) (J) but make sure that the geometry is right. If you plan to intercut with original colour neg, dupe by printing through the base. The CRI can then be printed on black and white or colour positive (K) as a cutting copy. Black and white reversal originals (L) can be duped on 16mm reversal (M) from which a reversal cutting copy can be made (N).

2. Colour neg: an alternative method

Colour neg originals (A) can be printed on colour interpositive (B). The processed interpos can be printed on colour inter neg (C) which can then be printed on colour or black and white stock to make the cutting copy. Using this method the geometry of the original remains unaltered.

83

Matching uncut original to edited cutting copy.

Negative Cutting: Principle

When the fine cut of the picture has been perfected the camera original can be matched to the edited cutting copy. This work can be done before a film soundtrack is dubbed but it is often best to wait until the dub has been completed in case any last minute changes are required. Once the camera original has been cut changes often cannot be made. As I have already mentioned, the work of matching original to cutting copy is known as negative cutting. It is a specialist's job, not usually done by the editor, and must be done with great precision. When you have perfected your final edited version you will normally send your cutting copy to a negative cutting specialist. Often the work is done in a laboratory neg cutting department.

Cutting by numbers

The negative cutter does not know your film and may well not be particularly interested in its subject. He (or she) is only concerned with the numbers on the edge of the film. The neg cutter will first log your cutting copy. He will wind through and make a note of the numbers on the edge of each shot you have used. Then he will wind through the camera original and take out the same shots. Using a sychroniser, which must be spotlessly clean and free of any attachments like magnetic sound heads, he will match original and cutting copy, shot for shot and cut for cut. He will do this by lining up the numbers on the side of the cutting copy with the identical numbers on the edge of the original checking two numbers each side to make sure before he makes a cut. Then he will join the master with cement and run on until he has a reel or reels of original exactly matching the edited version of your film. If a film only consists of cuts, and there are no dissolves, it is quite possible to neg cut a 16mm film in one reel so that at the end of the job you have one reel of edited cutting copy and one reel of edited camera original. Alternatively, the original can be assemoled in two rolls using either a checkerboard or A and B roll process.

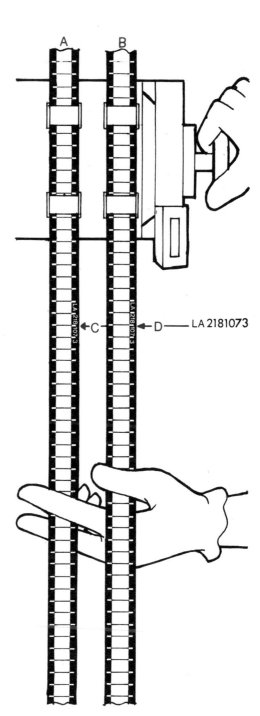

A B

C D LA 2181073

Cutting by numbers
Use a clean synchroniser
without magnetic sound
attachments and wear clean
white linen gloves. Put the
cutting copy (B) in the first
track. Wind down to the first
edge number. Take the
original for the same scene
and put it alongside in the
2nd track of the synchroniser
(A). Align the edge numbers
so that they are exactly
parallel (C & D). Wind on and
check another number to
make sure you have not made
a mistake, then wind back
and cut the original, level with
the cut in the cutting copy.
Join with cement.

85

Negative Cutting: Checkerboard

When films are printed on a single roll of edited original, a small white flash can sometimes be noticed where emulsion has been removed at joins. With checkerboard assemblies this flash can be eliminated. By using black leader between the shots and by overlapping the join in the direction of the leader which parallels the following shot on the opposite roll the white flash can be lost altogether. In the checkerboard system original and black spacing are assembled alternately on alternate rolls.

Starting a checkerboard assembly
If you have to neg cut original film and want to use the checkerboard system this is what you should do:
1. Wind through the cutting copy and log each shot, noting the edge numbers.
2. Extract the same edge numbered shots from the rolls of camera original. Hang them in a scrupulously clean trims bin or coil in individual rolls. You should wear white linen gloves before handling original material.
3. Ensure that the editing bench is clean and place a synchroniser free of magnetic sound attachments in the centre of the bench. Position a film horse on the left hand side and free unbent split spools on a rewind arm on the right.
4. Rewind the cutting copy and place it in the first track of the film horse and the first track of the synchroniser (the one nearest you) taking up the end of the first of the split spools.
5. Take two new leaders and place them in the second and third tracks of the synchroniser, level with the leader on the cutting copy. If the camera original is negative, use a negative leader. If it is reversal, use a suitable positive leader.
6. Scribe the name of the film on each leader, using a sharp pointed metal scribing pen. On one of the new leaders scribe "roll A" on the second scribe "roll B".
7. Join at least ten feet of white spacing on the start of both the new leaders. You can then take up the spacing on the second and third of the split spools and wind all three leaders down until you come to the first frame of picture on the cutting copy.

CHECKERBOARD
NEG CUTTING

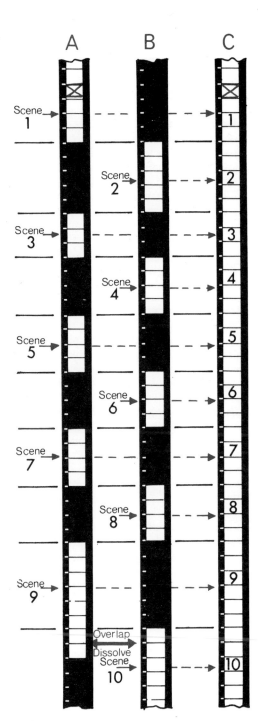

A   B   C

Scene 1

Scene 2

Scene 3

Scene 4

Scene 5

Scene 6

Scene 7

Scene 8

Scene 9

Overlap
Dissolve
Scene 10

Moving from roll to roll
The scenes in the cutting copy (C) are assembled in two separate rolls (A & B). Scene 1 goes on roll (A), scene 2 on (B) and so on. Use black leader between the shots and overlap the join in the direction of the leader which parallels the following shot to avoid the join flash. Do not forget the overlaps for opticals and wipes. Scene 9 dissolves to scene 10.

87

Negative Cutting: Where and When

Where the first frame of picture is joined to the leader of the cutting copy, you will have to join the same scene of camera original on either the A or the B roll matching edge numbers step by step.

Matching edge numbers step by step

Look at the first edge number on the first shot of the cutting copy. Mark one frame of it with a small wax pencil mark on the side of the film. Now find the same point on the same number on the camera original and put the two identical numbers opposite each other with the original in the fourth track of the synchroniser.

Wind down to the next edge number and check to ensure that the cutting copy and the original match exactly. When you are sure they do, wind back to the point at which the cutting copy leader is joined to the first frame of picture and mark the edge of the original film at that point. This is where you must cut. You can join it on to roll A, at the end of the leader.

Joining picture and leader

When you join the picture to the black leader, always keep the picture on the left hand side of the join. You must scrape the picture, not the black leader, otherwise the join will show. Always test the splicer before you make a join with original material to ensure that the blade is correctly lined up. You can not afford to tear the original film.

Checking numbers before making a cut

With the first shot now joined on roll A you can join black spacing on to roll B, at exactly the same point. Then wind down to the first cut in the cutting copy — the end of shot one and the start of shot two. At this point you cut out of shot one on the original and into shot two. You move from roll A on which you have placed shot one to roll B, joining black spacing onto the end of the first shot of roll A and joining the second shot onto the end of the spacing on roll B, at exactly the same point. Again, match the numbers on the shot and on the cutting copy by using the fourth, empty track of the synchroniser and then join so the joins on the cutting copy and on the A and B rolls are parallel. If the cutting copy consists only of cuts and there are no dissolves you can continue in this way to the end of the film.

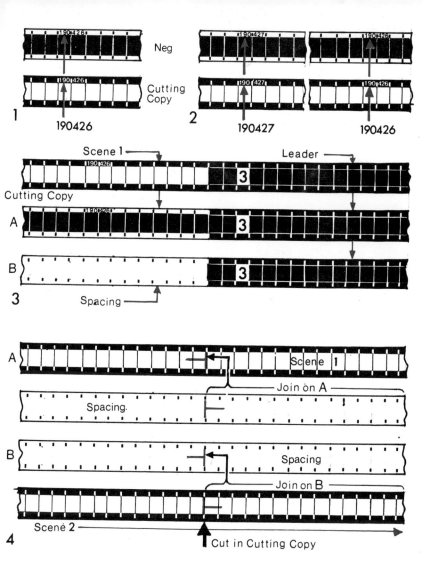

1

190426

2

190427 190426

Neg

Cutting Copy

Scene 1 — Leader —

Cutting Copy

A

B

3

Spacing —

A   Scene 1

Join on A —

Spacing.

B   Spacing

Join on B —

Scené 2 —

4   Cut in Cutting Copy

TARTING TO NEG CUT

irst steps

irst log the numbers of all the scenes in the cutting copy. Cut the complete
hots out of the original and hang them in a clean trims bin. Using a
ynchroniser (1) align the edge numbers of the start of the first shot. (2)
heck the next number. (3) Join scene 1 on to one leader (roll A) and black
pacing on to another leader (roll B). Wind down to the first cut. (4) Mark the
nd of the first shot on the spacing roll (B) and align the incoming shot. Cut
e incoming shot on to roll (B) and join spacing on to roll (A) at the same
oint.

Negative Cutting: Optical Effects

If your film contains dissolves you will need to overlap your cuts where the dissolves occur. This is not complicated. You still use alternate rolls for alternate shots but you must remember to allow the overlap we discussed earlier.

Overlapping checkerboard dissolves

Using the point at which you have joined the shots to be dissolved in the cutting copy as the centre of the dissolve you can join the first shot on the opposite roll to the shot which preceeds it, and run down to the centre point. Then, wind on, past the centre of the dissolve allowing half the length of the optical effect again: for example, an extra 24 frames beyond the point at which you joined in the cutting copy in the case of a 48 frame dissolve. You can then cut out of this roll and join on black spacing. Then wind back and join the incoming roll on 24 frames (in the case of a 48 frame dissolve) before the centre point, joining the incoming shot on the opposite roll to the outgoing one. Now check your joins.

You should find as you wind the film through the synchroniser the incoming shot starts on one roll 24 frames before the join in your cutting copy: the centre point of the dissolve. The outgoing shot, on the opposite roll, should continue for 24 frames after that centre point. Black spacing alternates with the shots on alternate rolls.

Marking centre points

You should also mark the centre of the dissolve with a small cross on each roll, opposite the join on your cutting copy. Scratch the mark on the edge of the emulsion side of the film between the sprocket holes but, obviously, away from the picture area, using a sharp scriber to scrape a small amount of emulsion off the film, thus leaving a clear and permanent mark. At the end of the process the join on your cutting copy and the two marks at the centre points on your A and B rolls should all be parallel in the synchroniser.

Assembling opticals for checkerboard printing may sound a long-winded process. In practice it takes around a minute to neg-cut a dissolve.

OVERLAPPING CHECKERBOARD DISSOLVES

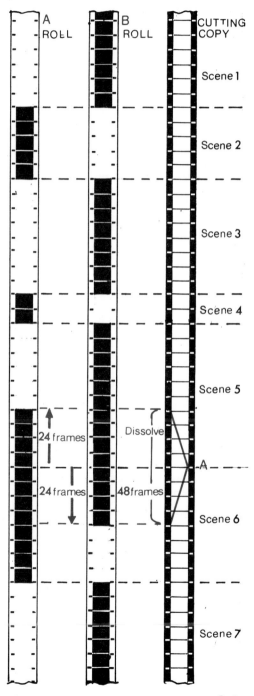

A ROLL

B ROLL

CUTTING COPY

Scene 1

Scene 2

Scene 3

Scene 4

Scene 5

Dissolve

24 frames

24 frames

48 frames

A

Scene 6

Scene 7

Allow half the length of the dissolve on each side

In this checkerboard assembly scenes change from (A) to (B) every time there is a cut. The joins on the A & B rolls are level with those on the cutting copy except where there is a dissolve (A). Here a 48 frame dissolve out of roll B into A requires an overlap of 24 frames on each side of the centre point. The incoming shot (A) is joined on 24 frames before and the outgoing one (B) carried through 24 frames after, the centre point. The laboratory will start to fade out B and fade in A at the same point. This technique enables dissolves to be printed directly from the original, so optimum quality copies should result.

Negative Cutting: A/B Rolls, Cueing

An alternative to checkerboard assembly, also using two rolls is the A and B roll method. The main difference is that instead of changing from roll A to roll B at every cut the change only needs to be made where there is a dissolve. For example, if your film is neg cut in A and B rolls but not checkerboarded, the original will be matched to the cutting copy by using numbers in the way already described. Only when the original is joined does the difference between A and B roll assembly and checkerboard become apparent. In the checkerboard system alternate shots are placed on alternate rolls—if scene one is on roll A scene two will be on roll B scene three on roll A and so on. When A and B roll assemblies are used, scene one may be on roll A and scene two, if it cuts on to scene one and does not dissolve into it, can also be joined onto roll A and so on until a dissolve is reached. The incoming shot of the dissolve can then be placed on roll B. The following shot can be joined again on roll B and continue until the next dissolve when the incoming scene can be placed on roll A. You only need to change from one roll to the other where two scenes must overlap. For practical purposes the checkerboard system, though taking slightly longer to prepare, is undoubtedly the best system to use. If you have to use it, you should use a frame line cement joiner making the smallest possible cement join (1/16th of an inch) overlapping each join towards the black leader which parallels the following shot on the other roll. You will thus ensure that the join is invisible.

Optical cue sheets
For fades in or out you do not, of course, need an overlap though you will need to tell the laboratory where they are to occur. When you are winding through to check the cut rolls of camera original, you zero the footage counter on the synchroniser at the point where the leader is joined to the first frame of the action. When you come to the start of the first optical, you make a note of the footage from the head of the roll. You should repeat this process as each optical starts so that when you reach the end of the roll you will have a complete list of the footages at which each optical effect occurs. This optical cue sheet should be sent with the cut camera original to the processing laboratory, when you order a print.

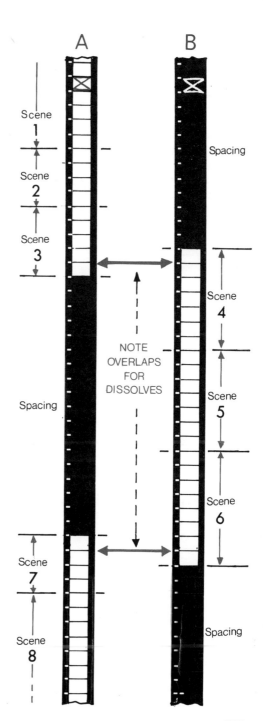

In an A & B assembly you only move from roll to roll when you need an overlap. Scene 2 cuts on to scene 1 and scene 3 on scene 2—all level cuts, so the original is cut and joined on the same roll (A). Scene 3 dissolves to scene 4 so an overlap is needed and provided by putting the incoming scene on a separate roll (B). 4 cuts on to 5 to 6, all on the same roll until the next dissolve—6 to 7—when we go back to roll A. Dissolves and wipes require an overlap. Fades do not, so you can keep shots requiring fades on the same roll.

93

Negative Cutting: Completing

Neg cutting checkerboard and A/B assemblies may sound complicated and time consuming. With practice it is simple and as optical effects are printed directly from the camera original the quality of resulting copies should be superb—far better than from any single roll duplicate.

Checking neg cut rolls

When you get to the end of your assembly rewind the rolls with great care and then replace the two assemblies in the synchroniser. It pays to wind through again, slowly checking each cut and each dissolve. You should not find any mistakes, but if mistakes have been made it is better to know about it now rather than send the reels off to a laboratory and possibly have to pay for a useless print. So check the whole film with the work print. If you find a mistake, putting the rolls out of synchronism, cut black spacing and adjust that, taking out frames or inserting new ones as necessary. Do not attempt to peel any of the joins between spacing and original. Do not cut or add to the picture. You may lose a frame when you make the join.

Additional C and D rolls

In the checkerboard and A and B roll systems described, the camera original is assembled in two separate rolls. For more complicated assemblies it is quite possible to add extra rolls. You might for example have an A, B, C and D roll, particularly if the camera original is filmed on reversal stock. You can then use the additional rolls to superimpose titles. You can neg cut the camera original in A and B rolls and make up one or two additional rolls (C and D) enabling titles to be overlaid. The laboratories will then print the backgrounds from the A and B rolls, superimposing the titles from the C and D rolls. The diagram shows how titles and backgrounds should be cut in the master rolls. We are using A, B, C and D rolls in this instance because the backgrounds dissolve with each other. Roll A dissolves to roll B and the first title dissolves to the second—roll C dissolves to roll D and so on. Note the overlaps.

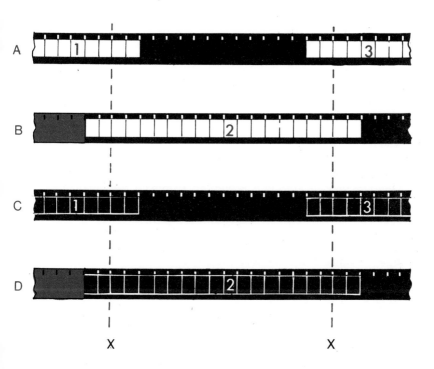

ADDITIONAL C & D ROLLS

Title assembly of reversal original using A, B, C, and D Rolls allowing for a
title to be superimposed over a moving background. Backgrounds and
letterings mix from one to the other. (A1) Background of the first title. (B2)
Background of second title. (A3) Background of third title. (C1) Lettering of
first title. (D2) Lettering of second title. (C3) Lettering of third title. (X and Y)
are centres of dissolves. Again, note the overlaps.

95

Superimposed Titles

Reversal originals
Titles can be superimposed on either reversal or negative original shots but they require differing techniques. When titles have to be superimposed over reversal original shots, title lettering should be shot on high contrast reversal film ready for superimposing. It is best to shoot white lettering on shiny black card. The necessary contrast can then be obtained in processing the lettering original. If the lettering is drawn on a dull black card, it will not be possible to obtain a sufficient contrast to enable the lettering to be superimposed satisfactorily over a film background. The dull black background may print as a dark grey and slightly fog the background over which the lettering is supposed to be superimposed.

Titles can be superimposed over reversal backgrounds when copies of the film are printed by assembling the camera original in A, B, C and sometimes also D rolls. The same technique cannot be used when the camera original has been shot on negative film. A duplicate negative must be made to incorporate the superimposed title.

Negative originals
If the film you are cutting was shot on 16mm colour negative and you want to superimpose lettering over a prefilmed title background, the procedure is as follows:

First the lettering must be drawn — again, plain white lettering on a glossy black card. The lettering can then be filmed, on black and white negative stock. The laboratory should be asked to process the negative and to make a maximum density print. At the same time, the original negative of the background must be removed from the uncut rolls of original and sent to the laboratory. They will make a low contrast print of the whole scene: a print known as an interpositive. They will then marry up the title and the background by simultaneously re-exposing the interpositive of the background and the high contrast print of the lettering on a. reel of new negative colour stock. This can then be processed and when the original negative of the film is cut, can be cut into it. Your responsibility as the editor is to provide the laboratory with the background material, with the lettering maximum density print and precise instructions for where to start the title and where to end it and where to start the background and where it, too, should end. You must tell them if you want the background to mix in or out or to fade in or out and if you want the lettering to cut in or fade in and out and so on.

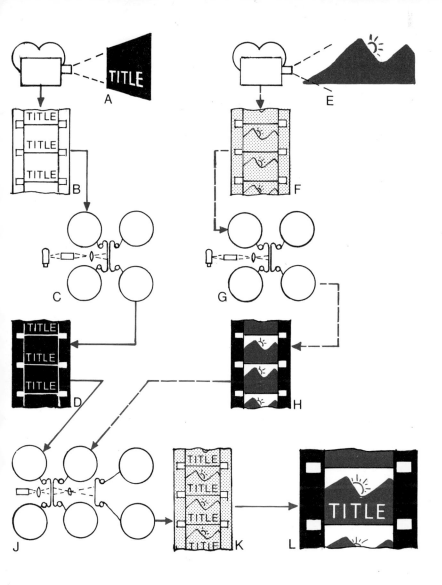

SUPERIMPOSING TITLES OVER NEG. ORIGINALS

(A) Title lettering should be white on glossy black card. Shoot on black and white neg (B). Make a maximum density print (C & D). The background (E) filmed on colour neg (F) can be printed (G) on colour interpositive stock (H). The maximum density lettering print (D) and background interpos (H) can then be optically printed together (J) on colour internegative stock (K). Lettering can be coloured at this stage. Finally, a cutting copy of the new optical neg can be printed (L). Some laboratories use a colour reversal negative process which replaces the background interpositive and gives better definition.

Ordering Superimposed Titles

When you have decided where you want titles and backgrounds to begin and end you can cut the shots you intend to use as backgrounds into your cutting copy in the normal way, using the rush print. Then you can turn your attention to the edge numbers and give the laboratory instructions by quoting the numbers at which you want titles to cut in and out or fade in and out and where you wish the backgrounds to change as well.

You must ask the laboratories to prepare a dupe incorporating the titles and you must supply them with precise details of what you want, listed on an optical instruction sheet. Here are some details from a typical instruction sheet:

Start background dupe at 29U976 $\boxed{18}$ — 4.
Start 20 frame fade in of title "Sorel Films present" at $\boxed{29}$ U97619 + 0.
Start 20 frame fade out of title only at $\boxed{29}$ U97621 — 10.
Cut out of background at 29U97 $\boxed{622}$ + 11.
Cut into background 29U $\boxed{46}$ 021 + 7.
At 29U4 $\boxed{60}$ 22 start 20 frame fade in of title "Peter Ustinov at Home".
29U460 $\boxed{24}$ + 7 start 20 frame fade out of title.
29U460 $\boxed{25}$ — 15 cut out of background.

In the example shown, we have faded the titles in and out and cut the backgrounds in and out. It is quite possible to mix from one title to another while superimposing the backgrounds. You can also mix from one background to another either at the same or at a different point. Specify exactly what you want to do by using the edge numbers on the side of the background film. You do not need to specify the numbers of the title lettering. The laboratories will then produce the necessary dupe.

Coloured lettering for titles

I have said that the lettering should be filmed on black and white stock, using white lettering on black card. This does not mean that the lettering on the finished titles can not be coloured. It is quite possible to tint the lettering when making the dupe. Yellow and red tints work particularly well on 16mm. When a film has been neg cut, the edited original can be returned to the laboratories and prints of the final version of the film can be produced. That is all as far as the picture is concerned but there is also the sound to be cut.

ORDERING
SUPERIMPOSED TITLES

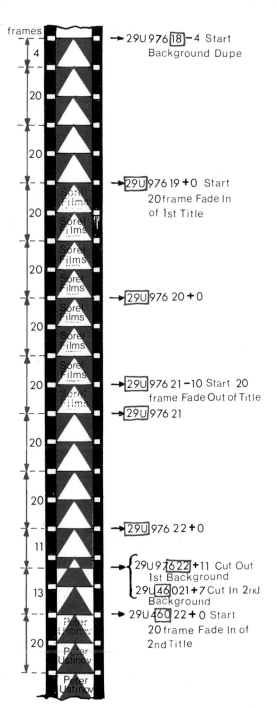

frames

→ 29U 976 18 -4 Start
Background Dupe

→ 29U 976 19 +0 Start
20 frame Fade In
of 1st Title

→ 29U 976 20 +0

→ 29U 976 21 -10 Start 20
frame Fade Out of Title

→ 29U 976 21

→ 29U 976 22 +0

{ 29U 976 22 +11 Cut Out
1st Background
29U 46 021 +7 Cut In 2nd
Background

→ 29U 46 22 + 0 Start
20 frame Fade In of
2nd Title

Edge numbers enable you to
give precise instructions to
the laboratory. Always dupe
complete shots and give
numbers for the start and end
of the background dupes and
for the start and end of
superimposition or optical
effects. Laboratories will
often provide pads of optical
order forms to help.

99

Synchronised Sound: Double System

In cutting a film you will also have to prepare the soundtrack. Again you must have suitable materials to work with.

Cutting sound
A 16mm film can be shot without any sound at all. Documentary films are often shot "mute". The whole soundtrack is prepared during cutting. An alternative is to shoot with synchronised sound. What is synchronised sound, and how is it filmed?

Synchronised sound exactly matches the picture to which it refers. If a shot shows a man hitting a nail with a hammer, the bang on the soundtrack will exactly match the point at which the hammer and the nail touch in the picture. But if you are cutting sound and picture on separate pieces of film, as is usually the case, you will find that they cease to match if you move either sound or picture independently. Sound and picture will then be "out of synchronism".

Double system shooting
Synchronised sound is normally recorded on a tape recorder locked to a camera by a synchronising pulse. There is not always a visible connection between the camera and the recorder. The camera generates a pulse (usually 50 or 60 cycles) which is recorded on the side of the sound recording tape. The sounds being recorded occupy the other side of the tape. When filming is complete the tape is re-recorded on perforated magnetic film and, once this is done, the pulse is used to keep tape and the magnetic film in synchronism. This system, shooting the picture on mute film stock and simultaneously recording synchronised sound on tape, is known as double system shooting. By using crystal synchronising apparatus it is possible to synchronise one recorder and a number of cameras. There are many possibilities and, having sound and picture on separate pieces of film, you will be able to enjoy far more cutting freedom. An alternative is single system sound shooting.

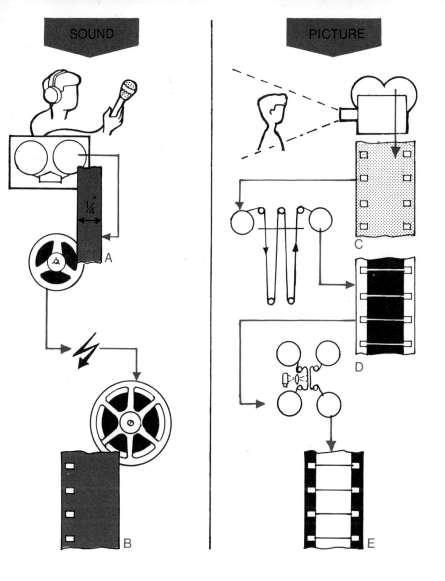

SYNCHRONISED SOUND; RAW MATERIALS TO WORK WITH

Double system shooting
Location sound is normally recorded on $\frac{1}{4}$in tape (A) locked to the camera by a synchronising pulse. After shooting, this pulse is used to govern the speed of a recorder re-recording the tape on perforated magnetic film (B) ready for cutting. Picture is normally shot on double perforated film (C) which must be processed (D). The processed original can then be contact printed on positive stock to make a rush print which can be used for cutting (E).

Synchronised Sound – Single System

In single system sound shooting, sound is recorded on a magnetic stripe along the edge of the picture film as it is being exposed in the camera. Magnetically striped stocks are available in both reversal and negative forms. Single system sound shooting is frequently used by TV news cameramen because it offers greater mobility. It can however present a number of problems in cutting.

Magnetic stripe sound advance
The intermittent film movement through the picture gate of a camera is controlled by a claw. The claw pulls film down frame by frame. Consequently a sound recording head can not be placed alongside the picture gate as the jerking movement of the film through the gate would make the sound unusable. The sound recording head is therefore placed far enough away from the intermittent movement to obtain a smooth passage of film over its surface. In a 16mm camera designed for shooting and recording on magnetically striped film, the sound head is positioned 28 frames ahead of the picture gate. So, the sound is always 28 frames ahead of the frame to which it refers. This sound advance limits your cutting freedom. Every time you cut you have to remember that the sound for the frame you are cutting is 28 frames further on. Cutting such combined magnetic film needs practice and never offers the creative freedom of cutting with a separate magnetic track in level synchronism.

The magnetic stripe can be transferred on to separate perforated magnetic film. You can then edit it in the same way as with double system sound. Single system shooting is most handy when the original has to be processed and used in a hurry – hence its adoption for television news. The procedure for most normal film making conditions is to shoot double system and make a copy of the camera original for editing, simultaneously re-recording the tape sound on perforated magnetic film ready for cutting.

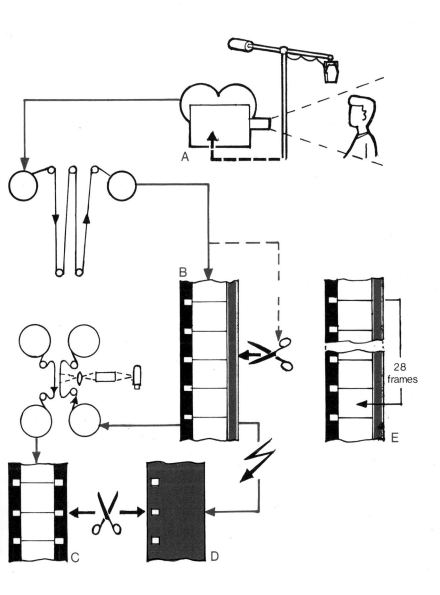

SYNCHRONISED SOUND

Single system shooting

Shooting on magnetically striped film stock (A). The processed film can then be edited using the magnetic striped sound (B). The sound will be 28 frames ahead of the picture and this can make cutting difficult (E). Alternatively you can have the magnetic stripe re-recorded on separate perforated magnetic film (D) and the processed original printed to make a mute cutting copy (C). You can then ignore the stripe track and cut in level synchronisation,

103

Cutting with Wild Sound

Often, 16mm films are shot without any sound at all. Others are shot without synchronised sound but with "wild" sound. What are "wild" sound tracks and what is involved in cutting a film shot with them or without any sound at all?

Sounds recorded on equipment working independently of a camera are known as wild tracks. Synchronised sound matches the picture exactly for it is recorded on equipment locked to the camera by a synchronising pulse. Wild tracks have to be synchronised in the cutting room. They cannot be synchronised accurately for long takes so there is no use in recording dialogue sequences wild. Wild tracks are normally used to provide background sounds — the sounds which are so important to the pace and life of every film. Look at any scene without sound. It lacks life. Sound effects are important. They can be obtained from sound libraries but the results will usually be better if wild tracks can be recorded when shooting is in progress.

Cutting with separate tracks
When a film is shot without sound or with wild tracks the picture will often be fine cut before a soundtrack is prepared. When you have perfected the picture you can start to prepare a soundtrack. You must prepare a number of different tracks, all matching the one edited version of the picture. Some will consist of sound effects, others narration and others music. Then, when all the tracks are prepared they can be mixed together in a dubbing theatre to make the one composite final mix master soundtrack audiences will hear with the finished film.

Wild tracks used with sync sound
Even when a film is shot with synchronised dialogue scenes, wild tracks should be recorded. The quality of synchronised dialogue scenes frequently varies slightly from shot to shot. During filming the changes are not always apparent but when the shots are cut together the difference is immediately noticeable. So you will need wild tracks of the background sounds to fill in the gaps. If the film has been shot without synchronised sound, you will have to use the wild tracks to build up your complete soundtrack. If wild tracks have not been recorded either, you will have to get the sounds you need from a sound effects library.

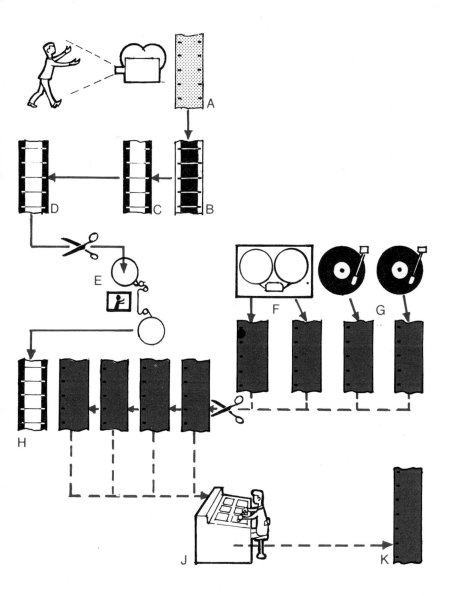

CUTTING WITH WILD TRACKS

Shoot on mute film (A). Process the original (B) and print a cutting copy (C).
Log rushes (D). Assemble and fine cut (E). Transfer tape wild tracks to
perforated magnetic film (F) and augment with music and sound effects from
tape/disc, all of which must be re-recorded on perforated magnetic film (G).
Cut the tracks to match the edited cutting copy (H). Dubb (J) to mix all the
tracks together making a final mix master magnetic soundtrack (K).

Planning a Complete Soundtrack

When the picture has been finalised sit down and look at it again and make a list of the sounds you need. Think first of sound effects. Analyse each scene in terms of sound. What will you need for the scenes on the facing page? It is useless to phone the library and request the sound of a car. They need to know what sort of car, what speed is it doing, whether it is stopping or moving forwards, or in reverse, if any doors open or close, where the car is, and what sort of background sound is needed. So, look at every scene and analyse it. Even a simple sequence needs a number of sounds to bring it to life. The scene opposite for example would have the following sounds:

1. **Exterior saloon car** (Ford Cortina 1975) stopping and engine switching off.
2. The same car. One door opening and shutting gently.
3. Man's footsteps on stone.
4. Background traffic — provincial town.

Breaking down sound
When you have listed the sounds you can ask the sound effects library to re-record their master tapes or discs on perforated magnetic film. You can then edit the film and build up a series of sound effects tracks, all matching the one edited reel of picture. You will need to prepare a number of different tracks. We can examine here just what the sequence of the car arriving and the man getting out and walking off means in terms of individual tracks. First, consider the background sound.

Start by running through the reels provided by the sound library and breaking them down into individual sounds. Hang them in a bin or coil them on reels. Identify the head of each with a wax pencil on the base side of the film. You can then turn to the synchroniser and the editing bench.

ASSESSING SOUND SCENES

Scene 1

Scene 2

Scene 3

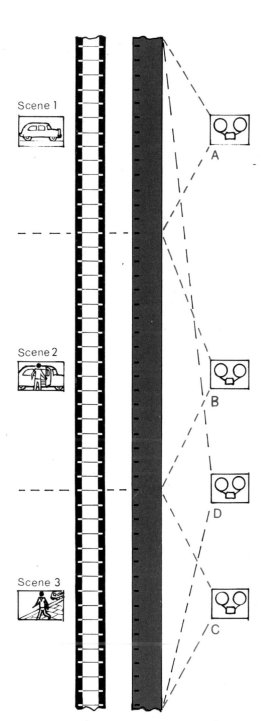

Analyse each scene

A car arrives and stops. A man gets out and walks away. You need four sounds to bring the scene to life. The sound of a car arriving and stopping (A). Car door opening and shutting (B). General distant traffic background atmosphere (D). Footsteps on stone paving (C). Transfer all these sounds to perforated magnetic film and lay on separate tracks.

Preparing Sound Effects Tracks

Take your reel of fine cut picture and put it in the first track of the synchroniser, nearest you. If you are using a fourway synchroniser this will leave you space for three soundtracks. It does not of course mean that your film can only have three soundtracks. You can prepare three, rewind and then prepare more. Put the cutting copy in the first track of the film horse and three reels of white blank leader in the other three tracks. Place the cutting copy leader in the first track of the synchroniser and take up the slack end on a split spool. Next you can take three new leaders and put them in the three empty tracks of the synchroniser. On the start of the first one you should write the title of the film and the words "Effects track 1, Reel 1 of 1-Head". On the start of the second one you should repeat the operation identifying it as Effects track 2 and likewise the third track as Effects track 3. You can then take up the ends of the leaders on split spools and wind on. Wind down to the start mark on the picture leader. Check that the other start marks on the other leaders are in level synchronisation — opposite the one on the picture. If they are, you can wind down to the first frame of picture.

Matching sound and picture
Wind down to the point where the leader on the cutting copy is joined to the first picture and, in exactly the same place, mark the ends of the other leaders. At this point you will start to join on sound or spacing. When you have marked it you can wind on, letting the three leaders on the tracks run out of the synchroniser. Now look at the first picture. It shows a car drawing up and stopping. Find the appropriate sound and put it in the second track of the synchroniser. You must synchronise the sound so that it stops at the same time as the car. Move the track about until it fits to a frame. Then wind back until you are opposite the first frame of the picture. Put a mark on the magnetic track parallel with the point at which the picture leader joins the first frame of the action — the point you have already marked on the other three leaders. Now you can make your cut, joining the track you have marked on to the first of your new leaders. For the time being join spacing onto the other two leaders. Then check all your joins to ensure that they are parallel with the join at the start of the cutting copy.

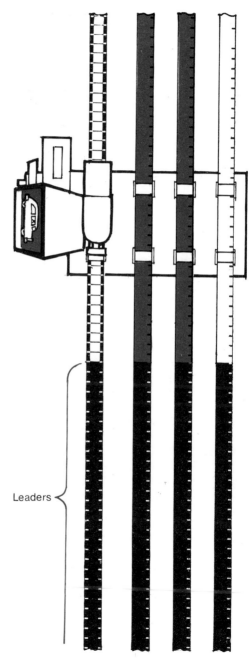

B   A   C   D

Leaders

Using separate tracks
The cutting copy (B) shows
the car arriving and stopping.
The sound of the car goes on
track (A) starting level with
the picture. A back up
atmosphere track of distant
traffic goes on a second track
(C) starting at the same point.
The third track (D) not needed
for this shot is built up with
spacing.

Preparing Background Sounds

So much for basic picture/sound synchronising. What about the other associated background sounds? You will need to use another track for background traffic noises. It is not a precise effect — the roar is the same all the time, so it can be joined in level with the first frame of picture. So, wind back to the first frame of picture and take another look at the synchroniser. You have the cutting copy starting in the track nearest to you, the track of the car stopping in the next track and spacing in the other two tracks. You want the traffic roar to start where the scene starts, so wind back and, joining on the left of the synchroniser, peel the join of the spacing to the third of the leaders and join on the background traffic sound in place of the spacing. You can then wind on again and check your joins. You should find that the start of the picture, the start of Track 1 and the start of the background traffic sound are all parallel in the synchroniser. Spacing remains on the last track. You do not need any more sounds for the first shot so you can wind down.

Joining spacing and magnetic
When you join spacing to magnetic film the base side of the spacing (the shiny side) should be joined in contact with the base side of the magnetic. This is an unusual practice. When you join picture to picture or magnetic to magnetic you always join so that the two base sides of the film are on the same side and the two emulsion sides likewise face the same way. Only when joining spacing to magnetic is the situation reversed. You join cel to cel: the cellulose base of the spacing in contact with the cellulose base of the track. Why is this change necessary?

Magnetic soundheads are tough. Magnetic soundtracks are designed to stand up to plenty of wear but the soft emulsion side of film spacing is not. It will scrape off and clog the soundheads, spoiling the sound and helping to wear them out. But the shiny side of spacing is tough enough to stand up to the soundheads. By joining base to base the tough side of the spacing faces the soundheads and synchronism can be preserved from scene to scene.

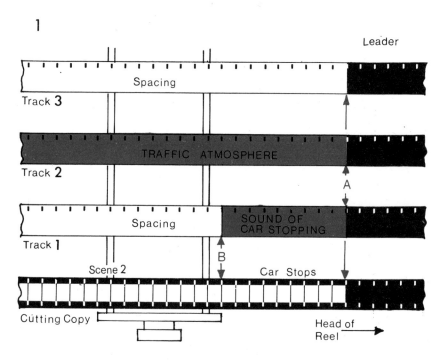

1

Leader

Spacing

Track **3**

TRAFFIC ATMOSPHERE

Track **2**

A

Spacing

SOUND OF
CAR STOPPING

Track **1**

Scene 2

B

Car Stops

Cutting Copy

Head of
Reel

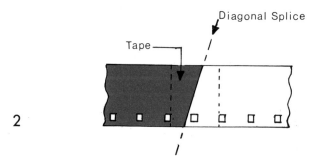

Diagonal Splice

Tape

2

USING SPACING WITH MAGNETIC

1. Where sounds are not needed, tracks can be built up with white spacing joined so that the shiny (cell) side of the spacing is the same way round as the dull side of the magnetic (contrary to normal picture joining practice). The spacing ensures that later tracks remain in synchronism from the head of the roll.

2. Diagonal join
When joining magnetic to magnetic or magnetic to spacing you can use either a straight or a diagonal join. Always use tape.

Sync Points

Now look again at the scenes with the man and his car. At the end of the first shot the car had stopped and the driver's door opened. There is the sound of a car door opening and closing, hanging in the trims bin, but how do you make it fit the picture?

Marking sync
First wind down the picture and mark the frame where the door opens with a cross. Now, before you do anything else, mark level synchronism on the picture, on the two soundtracks for the first scene and on the spacing all at the same point. You can use a wax pencil to mark one frame of picture and one frame of sound. A cross in a box is the customary sign to mark picture and three parallel lines are normally used on sound. You can then take the third track out of the synchroniser knowing that you will be able to resynchronise it by aligning the wax pencil marks.

"Laying" spot effects
Now, wind back to the point where the car door opens in the picture. You put a mark on that frame. Take the soundtrack for that particular sound and put it in Track 3 of the synchroniser. Wind down to the point where the sound of the car door opening begins. Mark that one frame with a cross. Then, take the track out of the synchroniser and re-align it, putting the cross on the track exactly parallel with the cross on the picture. Sound and picture are then in synchronism. Now you can join this sound into the spacing on Track 3, coming into it fractionally before the sound effect occurs. So, mark the point at which you want to cut into the sound and mark the same frame on the cutting copy. Now you can temporarily remove the track from the synchroniser. Wind back to your sync marks and re-synchronise the picture and the track you have already prepared. Wind down again to the mark on the picture at the point where you want the car door opening sound to start. Mark the spacing on track three at this point. You can now cut out of the spacing and into the sound at this point by joining on the two marks you have made, again making your join on the left of the synchroniser. This way of fitting sounds to picture is known as "laying sounds". Sounds which have to be accurately synchronised to frame like car doors, footsteps and hammer blows are known as spot effects.

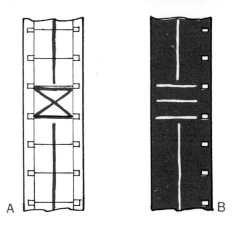

1   A   B

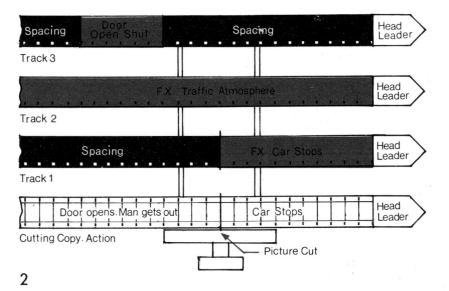

2

SAFEGUARDING SYNC

1. Sync marks
A wax pencil mark on one frame of sound and one of picture will enable you
to mark synchronism before making adjustments. A cross in a box is
normally used to mark picture (A); three parallel lines are frequently used on
sound (B).

2. Use separate tracks
If the recorded sounds are on separate tracks the sound mixer can adjust the
volume and pitch of each sound during dubbing. If the door on track 3 is too
loud or too quiet he can adjust it. The background atmosphere track (Traffic
on track 2) will cover the joins so that you cannot hear space cutting in and
out. Track 2 can run on until a change of location makes another background
atmosphere track necessary.

113

Matching Sound and Picture

We can now consider the sound of the footsteps of the man walking away from his car. You have in the trims bin the sound of a man walking on a stone pavement. How do you make the sound effects supplied by a sound library from a master recording match the movements of the man in your picture? Again you use a synchroniser. Wind down the picture and mark each frame with a cross. Mark one frame only — the frame where the man's feet and the pavement first meet for each step. That is the frame that makes the sound. Then, wind through the magnetic soundtrack and mark the back of the track with every footstep point. You can then put the first two crosses, one on sound and one on picture, opposite each other in the synchroniser and wind down.

Adjusting out of sync sounds
You will probably find that, although the first two crosses match exactly, the others are not so perfect. The man in the film shot was walking at a different speed from the man who made the master sound recording. So, you must make adjustments. You cannot cut the picture so you will have to adjust the track. If the sound is late, cut out the gaps between the steps on the soundtrack until each cross on the track is level with the cross on the picture. If the sound is early, you must space out the steps by inserting spacing in the track between the different paces. The soundtrack will go dead as the spacing passes over the soundheads but that does not matter for the other background tracks you have prepared will cover the gaps. With the crosses opposite each other on sound and picture the footsteps will be in precise synchronism. Sound and picture will match each other exactly.

Cutting to music
Music soundtracks can be laid in the same way as the effects tracks we have discussed. Alternatively, scenes can be cut to music. When music tracks are laid, the sound is made to fit the picture. When picture is cut to music, the pictures are cut to match the beat of the tune being heard. First run the film, marking the track with a wax pencil at the point where you wish to make your cuts. You can then cut the picture so the picture cuts match the marks on the back of the magnetic film.

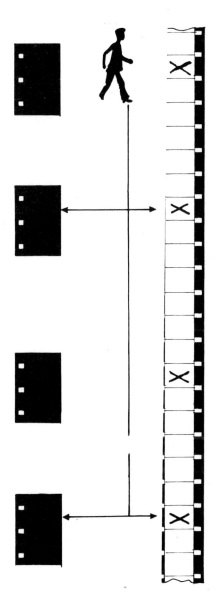

'LAYING' FOOTSTEPS

Accurate spacing of 'spot' effects
The man on your film is not walking at the same speed as the man who made the library sound recording, so adjustments must be made. Mark the sync point with a cross on picture then mark each footstep on the back of the magnetic with a one frame cross. Put the crosses opposite each other in a synchroniser and build up with spacing. A background atmosphere track must also be prepared.

Cutting Sounds and Avoiding Clicks

We have seen how to cut into the beginning of a sound but where should the sound end? You do not have to cut out of the soundtrack because the picture ends at that point. When you move from picture to picture you can make the transition by means of a cut or by a mix. The same applies to soundtracks. You can cut instantly out of one sound and into another or you can mix from sound to sound. You will need to provide a sound overlap where scenes dissolve from one to the other in the cutting copy and there are other occasions where the picture cuts but where a sound dissolve can enhance the feeling and mood of the film. Try to avoid cutting sound abruptly unless you are aiming to make a particular point. When you join magnetic tracks, use a tape joiner. It is best to choose one that makes a diagonal cut. Always mark your cutting points on the base side of the film and never on the side containing the sound recording. Do not use an overlap cement splicer on magnetic film. Cement may dissolve the oxide coating carrying the sound recording and leave you with a gap in your sound.

De-magnetising joins and joiners

Once you have marked your cutting point you can either make the cut straight away on a tape joiner or you can cut off the length you do not require, using a pair of demagnetised scissors or a razor blade. Obviously you will not get a precise cut with scissors. You can simply cut off the long length of surplus and then move to the joiner to make the precise cut you have marked. In making the join you will use the tape joiner and the techniques we have already discussed.

Tape joiners need degaussing from time to time. If they become magnetised you can hear joins click as they it pass over a sound head. They can be demagnetised by going over the joiner blade and block with a magnetic erasing pencil.If a join clicks you can sometimes remove the click by carefully aiming the point of the pencil at the join and drawing the magnetic field away from the film. This must be done with great care for a magnetic erasing pencil will erase anything it is allowed to come in contact with. You will only need to demagnetise a join if the joiner it is made on has been allowed to become magnetised. Normally magnetic film joins made with tape, using a diagonal join, require no after treatment.

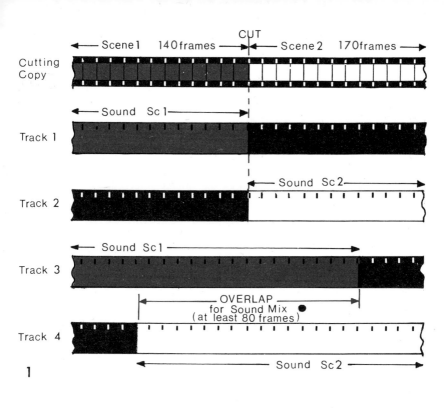

1

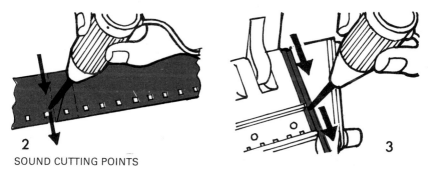

2

3

SOUND CUTTING POINTS

1. Moving from scene to scene

You can cut, mix or fade sound level with the picture or at a different point. Tracks 1 and 2 are laid for a cut. The sound changes at the same point as the picture. Tracks 3 and 4 offer an alternative. They are laid with an overlap so that the sounds can be mixed together.

2. Degaussing magnetic clicks

Unwanted clicks can often be removed by moving an erasing pencil gradually across and away from the film.

3. Degaussing tape joiners

Joiners can become magnetised and put clicks on joins. By moving a degaussing pencil across and away from the joiner cutting blade the magnetic field can be drawn away.

Background Sound Loops

Sometimes you may find that there is a non sync sound effect you want to use at various points throughout the film. It might perhaps be a general background traffic noise or the sound of distant sea. Sound effects of this kind can sometimes be made into a continuous loop. You can loop a sound effect to make more space on the laid tracks for other sounds. But loops should be an exception rather than the rule. Wherever possible lay every sound on your various effects tracks. Sometimes, when you are working in a rush, you may find you have missed out a background sound or you may need to introduce yet another track simply for one background effect. In cases like this a loop can sometimes suffice. Do not go into a dubbing theatre with a series of loops and no laid tracks and expect the dubbing mixer to give you a welcome. Loops should only be used to cover gaps and to provide background atmosphere where laid tracks cannot be provided.

Preparing a sound loop
When constructing a loop, take care not to include anything which is over-obvious. If you have one outstanding effect it will be noticed every time the loop goes round. For example, in the case of a loop of country atmosphere, avoid any obvious bird song. And make the loop long enough to avoid being markedly repetitive. All you have to do is record a length of the sound you want to loop. Pick two points where the recording levels are identical and join them end to end with a diagonal tape join, making sure the loop is not twisted. Many dubbing theatres have their own small libraries of permanent loop effects. Often these are on cassette quarter-inch tapes. The loops you prepare yourself should be on perforated magnetic film, just like your laid tracks. You know the dubbing theatre you are going to use can project 16mm perforated magnetic soundtracks. If you make up a tape loop you may arrive and find that they have a casette recorder or some type of machinery unable to cope with the loop you have prepared. Using 16mm film you are safe.

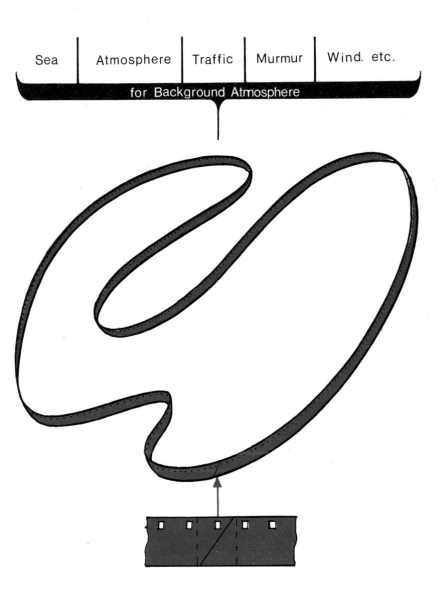

| Sea | Atmosphere | Traffic | Murmur | Wind. etc. |

for Background Atmosphere

LOOPED SOUND EFFECTS

General background sounds can sometimes be looped for continuous running. Avoid sounds where repetition would be noticeable and use a diagonal join when you make up the loop, joining at points where the recording level is identical.

Synchronised Sound and Picture

We have so far considered ways by which non sync tracks can be synchronised to picture in the cutting room. If the film you are cutting has been shot with synchronised sound for every scene you will be able to cut sound and picture simultaneously using either a synchroniser or a motorised editing machine. Comparatively few films are shot with sync sound for every scene and you will often find that you have some sound shots and some which are mute. We have seen how you prepare sound effects for the mute shots. How do you handle sync sound takes in the cutting room?

Synchronising rushes

After logging the rushes you must first synchronise sound and picture. First refer to the sound and camera report sheets and see which scenes have been shot with synchronised sound and which have not. Next, wind down the picture film on a synchroniser and find the start of the first synchronised sound take. If the camera crew have done their job properly there will be a clapper board (often referred to as a slate) on either the head or the end of the take. If it is at the end it should be held upside down. When you see a board upside down you will immediately know that it refers to the scene which precedes it and not the one which follows. To synchronise sound and picture, wind the picture down and find the point where the two parts of the board actually bang together. When you have found the precise frame — it will only be one frame — mark it with a wax pencil cross. The parts of the board may remain together for several frames but that does not really concern us. We are concerned with the frame where the two parts first bang together — the point where the sound is produced. Find that frame and mark it with a one frame cross, using a wax pencil. Alongside the cross note the shot and take number.

Next, temporarily ignore the picture and turn your attention to the track of separate perforated magnetic sound. Wind it, too, down on the synchroniser and listen until you hear the sound identification of the same shot. You should hear someone say "Scene 10 Take 1", or whatever it is, followed by a bang — the bang where the two parts of the board were actuallly banged together. Identify that one precise frame and mark it with a cross. All you have to do now is put the cross on the soundtrack and the cross on the picture alongside each other in two tracks of the synchroniser and wind down. Sound and picture should now be synchronised.

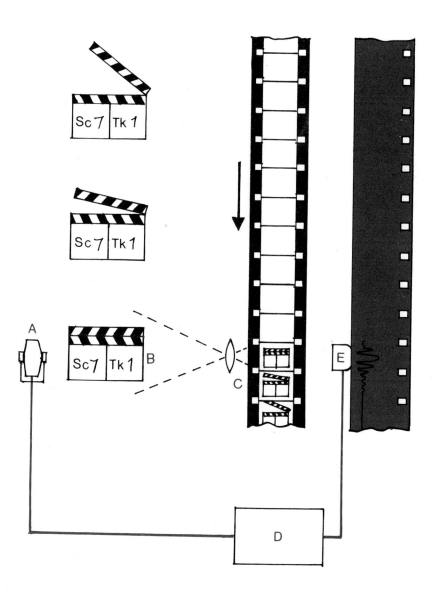

SYNCHRONISING RUSHES

An assistant reads scene and take numbers and bangs the two parts of the clapper board together. The point at which the top and bottom of the board first bang together (B) is recorded by the camera lens (C). A microphone (A) simultaneously records the sound. Sound reaches the film (E) via an amplifier (D). To synchronise sound and picture align the one frame where the board first bangs together with the frame where the sound bang starts.

Finding and Maintaining Synchronism

Some modern cameras employ an automatic sync marking device. When the camera has run up to speed a light built into the camera automatically fogs a small number of frames and a bleep is simultaneously reproduced on the sound recording. The exact system used tends to vary from one make of equipment to another. However, you will frequently find that where automatic synchronising equipment has been used the camera crew shooting the material have not bothered to provide clapper board identification. You will have to synchronise sound and picture by aligning the bleep on the sound with the clear frames on the picture. You will still need a clear aural identification of the sound shot. You can then often synchronise sound and picture by aligning the end of the bleep on the sound with the end of the clear (fog) frames of the picture. Automatic sync systems are notoriously unreliable. A weak camera battery can move the sync point by several frames so, though I have recommended aligning the last fogged frame of picture with the end of the sync bleep, this should not be regarded as a hard and fast rule.

Intercutting sync and mute takes

If the film you are cutting has been shot with synchronised sound for every scene you will be able to cut sound and picture simultaneously, using either a synchroniser or a motorised editing machine. Comparatively few films are shot with sync sound throughout and you may well find that you have some shots which are sync and some which are mute. How do you join the two together? Again you should use a synchroniser or a motorised editing machine, cutting sound and picture simultaneously whenever synchronised sound shots are involved. Where there is no sync sound, cut the picture on its own and build up the soundtrack by using spacing. Spacing makes no sound and if you use the same length of spacing as the mute shots in your reel of picture, synchronised sound shots on either side of the gap will remain in synchronism. In the example shown on the facing page, the film starts with a synchronised sound take. Then there is a mute sequence. The soundtrack has been built up by using spacing. When the next synchronised sound scene begins we have cut out of the spacing and into the sound again. Spacing ensures that the sound remains in synchronism from the head of the roll.

INTERCUTTING SYNC
AND MUTE TAKES

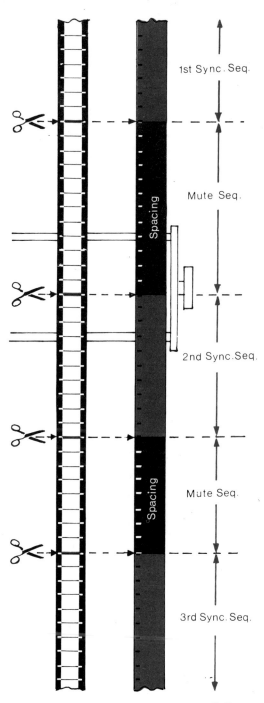

1st Sync. Seq.

Mute Seq.

Spacing

2nd Sync. Seq.

Mute Seq.

Spacing

3rd Sync. Seq.

Where sync and mute scenes
are intercut, spacing should
be used to preserve
synchronism from the head of
the roll.

123

Narration: Pre-Recording, Matching

We have so far considered synchronised sound, and music and effects tracks but we have not discussed voice over narration. Off-screen narration (commentary) is used in many films, particularly documentaries. It can be recorded at one of two stages of production. You can either record "to picture" during a dub or you can pre-record commentary and edit it to match the picture in the cutting room.

Pre-recording commentary

If you decide to pre-record and edit the commentary there is no need for the commentator to see the picture at all. Perhaps it is not even ready. The commentator sits in a recording theatre and reads the script, pausing at the appropriate punctuation marks. The film director will supervise the recording and ensure that the right commentary points are emphasised. At the end of the recording session you will have a reel of perforated magnetic film containing the unedited commentary. The first thing to do is to make a safety copy. You can re-record the master recording on either quarter inch tape or on another roll of perforated magnetic film. You will probably never need to use the safety copy but you should make one just the same. You will edit the actual recording and if you damage it and do not have the safety copy the commentator will have to be brought in again to re-record the sentences you damaged. And that will add to the production cost. You can take the reel of recording back to the cutting room and cut it to match the picture. You will do this again in a synchroniser. If you want to extend a pause in the commentary you simply cut the track and join in spacing. If the picture does not fit exactly at this stage you can still adjust it so that, at the end of the operation, picture and sound should match exactly. By pre-recording and laying commentary in this manner you have complete control.

When commentaries are pre-recorded you will find that sometimes the commentary needs to be matched to the picture and sometimes the picture to the commentary. By recording at this early stage you can make cuts to picture and sound. You will not have laid your sound effects tracks so you will not have to adjust them every time you make a picture cut. If you record later you will have less control.

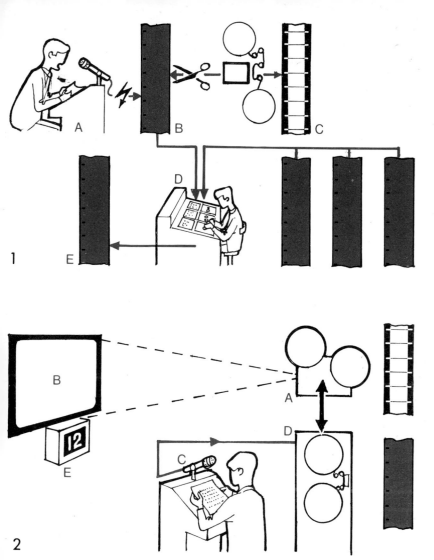

RECORDING VOICE/OVER NARRATION

1. Pre-recording

Record wild (A) on perforated magnetic film (B). Cut the recording to match the cutting copy (C) then augment the basic commentary by preparing music and effects tracks. The tracks can then be mixed together in a dubbing theatre to make a final mix master recording (E).

2. Recording to picture

Project your edited cutting copy (A) on a screen with a footage counter nearby (E). The narrator can read from a script taking his cues either from the footage counter or from a cue light (C). Record on perforated magnetic film (D). You can then immediately dub the new track with other tracks to make a final mix. Always keep narration on a separate track. A music and effects premix, free of narration, will simplify the process of preparing foreign versions.

Narration: Recording During a Dub

If you record narration 'to picture' you will record when the final edited version of the picture has been finalised and the other soundtracks have been prepared. You should record before you mix the other tracks together, making the commentary recording on a reel of new stock. The commentator can sit in a soundproof commentary compartment in the dubbing theatre. This time he can see the edited version of the film projected on a screen in front of him and he will have to read at exactly the right places. You can cue him for speaking by using a cue light and by listing the footages of the film alongside the paragraphs of his script. There is always a film footage counter under the screen in a dubbing theatre. This method of recording during a dub is widely used. It is a great time saver and, if the commentary writer is used to writing the correct number of words for a set period of time, there should not be any problem. For optimum accuracy it is best to pre-record and edit.

Dubbing procedure

When you have prepared all the different soundtracks you need you must make out a dubbing cue sheet, and take the tracks into a dubbing theatre so that they can be mixed together. The equipment in the dubbing theatre usually consists of a projector, locked to a number of sound reproducing channels and to one recording machine recording on 16mm magnetic stock. The various machines are synchronised to run together. They will normally run forward or in reverse, and remain in synchronism. When you dub, your cutting copy will be laced on the dubbing theatre projector and the separate magnetic soundtracks you have prepared will be laced on the various sound reproducing machines. A reel of new perforated magnetic film stock will be laced up on the recorder. The output of the tracks you have prepared will be fed to the recorder via a mixing console equipped with volume controls and sets of filters for each track. The man on the console (the dubbing mixer) blends your tracks together. He will take his cues from the picture projected in front of him, from your dubbing cue sheets and from a film footage counter under the screen. The various soundtracks he mixes together are recorded on one single track — the final mix master sound recording.

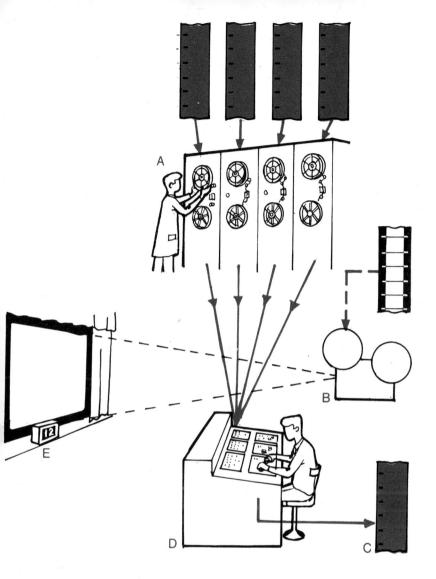

DUBBING PROCEDURE

In a dubbing theatre magnetic recording machines which will reproduce your separate magnetic sound tracks (A) are linked to a projector (B) which will show your edited cutting copy. A footage counter (E) is also locked into the system. Output of the tracks is fed to a console (D) where the sound mixer adjusts the pitch and volume of each track and mixes all the tracks together to make a final master recording on perforated magnetic film (C).

127

Dubbing: Procedure

Although you will prepare the soundtracks which have to be dubbed the mix will be done by a dubbing mixer. He does not know your film or your tracks so you must tell him what each track consists of and how you want each sound to start and end. The normal way to do this is to use a dubbing cue sheet.

Dubbing cue sheets

Cue sheets are divided into columns — one column for each track and one for action cues. At the top of the sheet you should write the title of the film and the reel number. The rest of the sheet should be used to tell the mixer about your tracks. List each track and show where you want each sound to start and end. If you want sound to cut in, draw a straight line across the column referring to the track. Starting footages should go above the line at the start of the sound and finishing footages beneath the line at the end of it. So, on the cue sheet illustrated, at $10\frac{1}{2}$ft Track 1 cuts in, at 14ft it cuts out. It is normal practice to measure the footages from the first frame of picture, right at the end of the leader.

If you do not want sound to cut in or out you can arrange for it to be faded in or mixed with other sounds. To mark a fade in you use an elongated letter V the wrong way up. The narrow part is where the fade in will start. The wide part indicates the point at which the sound will be fully faded up. So, at 14ft Track 4 starts to fade in, and by 16 feet it is fully up. If you use a V the other way up as I have done on Track 2 at 45 feet you will be indicating a fade out. So, on Track 2 at 45 feet a fade out begins and is completed by 47ft. If you fade out one track and simultaneously fade in another you are in effect mixing from one track to another. This is known as a cross fade (or a cross mix). At 36ft we cross fade from Track 3 to Track 4.

You will notice that the commentary of the film shown on the cue sheet has been pre-recorded and laid to picture. The commentary is Track 1. Always keep commentary on a separate track. It will make the mixer's job easier and if you want to make foreign language versions it will help you to pre-mix the other tracks. When you mark the commentary on a cue sheet it is worth writing the last words of each sentence before the out-point in each case.

DUBBING CUE SHEET

"FIRE AT WORK" Reel 1 F2   16mm FT: ZERO 1ST FRAME.

	1 COMM	2	3	4	LOOPS
C.U. TELE-PHONE.		01 TELEPHONE DIAL 6FT	6FT		
TELE EXCHANGE	10½	9½	TELE EXCHANGE ATMOS: 9½		
CONTROL ROOM	"ON FIRE" 14	FIRE CONTROL ROOM ATMOS: 24	— — — 24	14 16 TELEPHONE RINGING 24	
BIG FIRE	25 "ADVOIDED" 26	24 26	EXT: BURNING HOUSE. 28	28	
WALL CRASHES	32½	28 FIRE ENGINE APRRO 31	28 31	EXT: BURNING HOUSE (CLOSER) 31	
TITLES	"WHOSE FAULT" 37	43 CAR START 45 + AWAY 47	TELE: EXCHANGE ATMOS: 36 38 47 EXT: BURNING HOUSE 53	36 38 MUSIC 47 49	51 EXT: 53 ATMOS

DUBBING CUE SHEETS

Cue sheets can be vertical or horizontal. They should state whether each sound cuts in and out and give instructions for mixes and fades using footages to indicate the starting and finishing points. Straight lines indicate cuts. Track 3 cuts in at 47ft and out at 53ft. A fade indicated on track 4 starts at 36ft. It is fully faded in by 38ft. The same track fades out between 47ft and 49ft. Footages are normally calculated from the first frame of picture, hence 'zero first frame'.

129

Dubbing: Practice

Look at the composition of the tracks outlined on the cue sheet. On the facing page you can see what the opening sequences look like in a synchroniser. Compare them with the cue sheet. You can see that where there is no sound on a particular track it is built up with spacing. Note, too, how the sounds sometimes overlap. There are some sounds which come up on cue like the spot effects we have already discussed. There are others which become available, to be crept in as required. On the cue sheet Track 3 faded out at 38ft but the sound on the track runs through for longer giving the mixer an overlap, i.e.: room for manoeuvre. However, where the sound cuts in, as on Track 2 at 01 feet the point is exactly the same on the tracks and on the footage on the cue sheet.

M & E premix

If you have a large number of tracks to mix, the dubbing mixer will often pre-mix a number of them and then run through again blending the pre-mix with the remaining tracks. If you expect to produce foreign versions of the film you are cutting, you should pre-mix the music and effects tracks before adding the voice-over narration. The pre-mix track of music and effects, known as an M and E track, can then be mixed with narration tracks in any language.

At the end of a dubbing session you will have all your soundtracks mixed together on one reel — the master final mix. You may also have a master M and E (music and effects mix) and you will have the final edited cutting copy. The cutting copy can now be sent off for neg cutting. What do you do with the final soundtrack?The work of cutting is now almost completed. One stage remains — the preparation of the first showprint of the final edited film. The picture can be printed from the cut reels of camera original when they have been neg cut, but what about the soundtrack? You will probably want to prepare prints combining sound and picture.

There are two main kinds of combined print. One has an optical, photographic soundtrack and the other has one recorded on a magnetic stripe on the edge of the print. Magnetically striped soundtracks are usually of much better quality. Unfortunately there are comparatively few projectors capable of projecting magnetically striped copies. Optical sound prints are far more common.

COMPOSITION
OF TRACKS

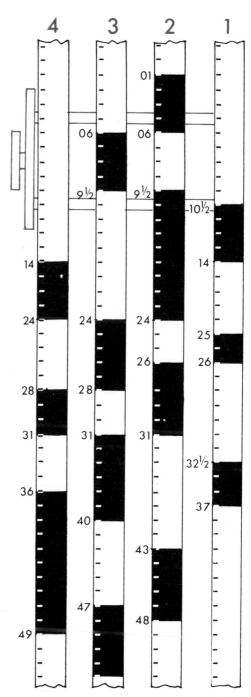

Where mixes occur
soundtracks, like optical
effects, need an overlap.
Track 3 mixes to track 4
between 36ft and 38ft (see
preceding cue sheet). The
editor has left an overlap
ending at 40ft. If you do not·
want sounds to cut in and out
instantly, always allow plenty
of overlap and cue
accordingly.

Combined Prints : Magnetic or Optical

To make a magnetically striped print you must first ask a laboratory to prepare a mute print on single perforated stock. You can then arrange for a coating of ferrous oxide to be applied to the edge of the film opposite the sprocket holes. The master magnetic final mix, recorded in the dubbing theatre, can then be replayed on one machine and simultaneously re-recorded on the magnetically striped print. Care must be taken to record the track with the correct sound advance as we shall see in a moment. This laborious process has to be carried out for every single print. Combined optical sound copies are easily produced in bulk. They are also considerably cheaper.

Magnetic stripe and optical sound compared

To make optical sound combined prints, the master magnetic final mix must first be re-recorded as a photographic optical sound negative. The negative, when processed, can be synchronised and printed with the editied camera original on positive stock. Optical soundtracks are visible. You can see fluctuations on the edge of the film. A recording on a magnetic stripe is invisible. You can see the stripe but you can not see the sound modulations. The sound can only be heard by replaying it via a magnetic soundhead.

Sound advance

We will begin by considering the term "sound advance". If you look at any 16mm film projector you will notice that the sound head and picture gate are separate. The film runs from a feed reel through the picture gate and on round a sound drum out to the take-up reel. Sound and picture are thus separated. This is because movement through the picture gate is intermittent. The picture is advanced frame by frame by a claw. Movement round a *sound* drum however, must be smooth at a constant speed if the quality of the sound is to be acceptable. The distance between the picture gate and the sound head is known as the sound advance. For 16mm optical sound combined prints the sound must be advanced 26 frames. For 16mm magnetically striped prints, the sound must be advanced 28 frames.

Combined optical sound copies, are known as "comopt" copies, and magnetically striped copies as "commag". When picture and sound are on separate pieces of film the terms "sepmag" or "double headed", are generally used.

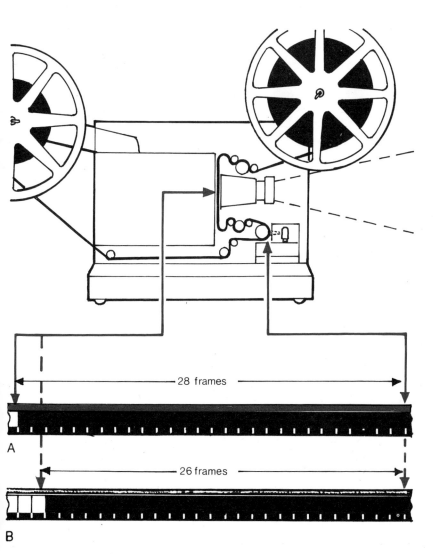

28 frames

A

26 frames

B

COMBINED PRINTS: SOUND ADVANCE

Sound and picture separation

Projector picture gates and soundheads are separated by a set number of frames. The number is internationally standard, so films made in different countries are interchangeable. On a 16mm combined magnetic sound film (A) the sound is advanced by 28 frames. On 16mm combined optical prints (B) the sound is 26 frames advanced. Movement through a picture gate is intermittent. Movement round a soundhead must be smooth. The sound advance ensures that sound and picture can both be satisfactorily reproduced.

Combined Prints: Optical Sound

How do you make a sound negative and prepare it for printing? You must first send the master magnetic track off to a sound recording studio to be "transferred" to optical sound. Before you send it off, you must mark an audibly recognisable point by replacing one frame of the leader with a frame of thousand cycle tone. You might perhaps remove the figure 3 on the leader and replace it with a frame of tone. This frame will reproduce as a bleep — and will give you a point to refer to on the sound negative. The bleep will immediately be recognisable as one frame of closely spaced lines.

Comopt copies : advancing sound for printing

When the optical sound neg has been developed and delivered to you in the cutting room you will have to synchronise it to the neg cut camera original. To do this you will need to use a synchroniser, a cement joiner and work at the cutting bench. Now you must remember where you put the frame of tone on the leader of the master magnetic. You replaced the figure 3 on the leader with a frame of thousand cycle tone. So, look for that frame on the sound negative. Remember it will appear as one frame of closely spaced lines. When you have found it, put it in the synchroniser opposite the figure 3 on the leaders of the picture film. Sound and picture are now in level synchronisation, as they were in the dubbing theatre. But remember, sound must be advanced on a combined print. So, take the optical sound negative out of the synchroniser and move it 26 frames towards the head of the roll. It is now in synchronism for 16mm comopt printing. Wind back to the start of the roll and mark start marks on the head of all the rolls writing the words "16mm printing sync — start — roll one of one — head". You can then wind carefully through to the end of the film and put end synchronism marks on as well identifying them as "16mm printing sync end. Reel one of one". Sound and picture can then be sent off to the laboratory for printing.

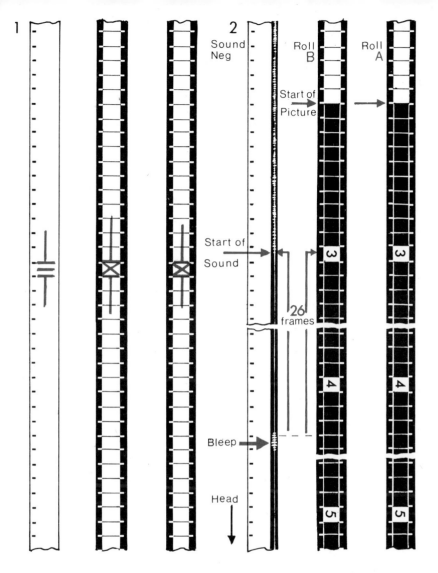

PREPARING COMBINED SOUND COPIES

1. Level synchronisation
The A & B rolls shown are in level synchronism with the magnetic track. Before you can make a combined optical sound print the magnetic must be re-recorded and the resulting sound neg advanced.

2. Advancing optical sound for printing
The tone on fig 3 of the leader appears as a visible bleep. For printing it must be advanced by 26 frames. Using a synchroniser, put the bleep opposite '3' and then move the sound neg 26 frames towards the head of the roll. Put "start" marks on the camera original and the sound neg marking them "16mm printing sync, Start". Comopt copies can now be printed.

135

Preparing the First Show Copy

The first print made from cut camera originals is known as an answer print. The laboratory will first grade the original. They will look at each shot and assess the printing exposure needed.

Grading 'answer' prints
As already mentioned, a film printing machine is rather like a camera. Light is allowed to pass through the master film onto a reel of new stock, thus re-exposing one on the other. The intensity of the light can be controlled by a shutter. The laboratory grader will assess the exposure needed for each shot. He will also assess any colour correction, grading the colour balance shot for shot. He will ensure that where you have cut from a medium shot to a close-up on the same subject the colours and the lighting conditions are the same in both shots. Today, there are machines to help with this work.

Automatic grading
Today graders often use closed circuit colour television analysers. They wind through the camera original and check it shot by shot. The analyser projects a picture from the original on a closed circuit television screen and the grader can test the various light and colour filter possibilities instantly. By flicking a switch he can change from one printer light to another and by looking at the television monitor screen he can see what the results would be on a print. He can also test the various colour filters combinations. He assesses the filters and light required for each shot and plots the results on a card. On many modern printing machines the card is then translated onto punched computer tape, which subsequently guides the film printing machine. Colour analysers have done much to revolutionise the work of the grader but the ultimate success still depends on the quality of your original and on the skill of the man doing the job. When the first print (the answer print) has been made it will be sent to you for checking. It should be good but it will rarely be perfect. There are usually some adjustments to be made in later prints.

Colour analyser
When the original film has been neg cut, it is put on a split spool on (A) and laced round a guide roller (B) — to the picture gate (C). The film is scanned by a flying spot cathode ray tube at (C) and the transmitted light is subsequently separated by dichrioc mirrors into red, green and blue components controlled by exposure and balance controls (E). The resulting signals are fed to a video display (D) where a positive image of the original material, either negative or positive, is produced. By experimenting with the controls, various colour filter and print density combinations can be tried until the correct grading for each scene is determined. Some models enable A & B rolls to be graded simultaneously.

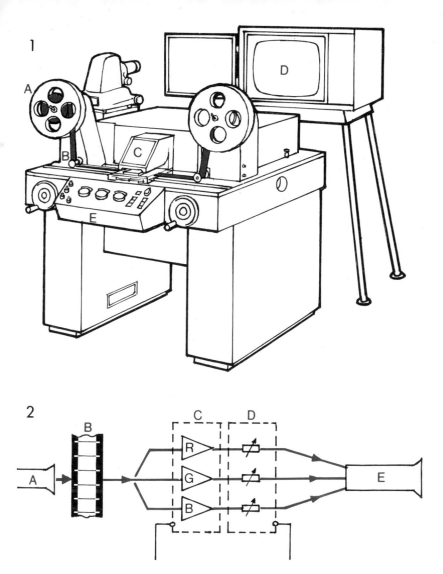

COLOUR GRADING

1. Colour analisers
The camera original (A) is wound via guide roller (B) past a scanning head (C). A positive image is displayed on a colour TV monitor screen (D) via a closed circuit TV system. Calibrated control knobs on the panel (E) enable a grader to try various density and colour filter combinations whilst seeing the results instantly in front of him on the screen. A still projector is sometimes used to project a reference picture on the adjoining screen.

Individual colour control
The picture relayed from scanner (A) reading the original film (B) is divided by dichroic filters into red, green and blue components. There are separate controls (D) for each colour. The signals are then processed to produce a colour positive image on the screen.

Prints Out of Sync

When you check the answer print make sure that you are checking it under the best possible conditions. Remember that you are checking sound as well as picture. When you run the film, look and listen for possible faults.

Sound out of sync

The sound may be out of sync with the picture. If it is, right from the start of the roll, the fault may be yours or that of the processing laboratories. Perhaps you made a mistake when you put the sound negative in printing synchronism with the camera original. Did you clearly mark the start of the film as being "in 16mm printing sync". If you did not, the laboratory may have assumed that sound and picture were in level synchronism and they may have advanced the sound a further 26 frames. If you did synchronise sound and picture in the correct manner the laboratory may have laced their printing machine incorrectly. If they have made a mistake they should reprint at their cost. If the mistake is yours you will have to make adjustments and pay for the reprint.

Tracing the source of faults

If the sound is only out of sync in a few places and not out throughout the entire roll, the error may be due to faulty negative cutting. Check the edited camera original against your cutting copy to ensure that they match exactly cut-for-cut and frame-for-frame. If you can not find a mistake in the neg cutting run your cutting copy with the final mix master magnetic soundtrack and then check the sound negative against the magnetic track. You may find that the soundtrack is in synchronism but is not of very good quality. Perhaps the sound is not loud enough. There may be an excessive background hiss. If this is the case, ask the laboratory to check the density of the optical track on the print. You should also check the optical sound negative. If the negative is faulty you will have to make a new sound negative by re-recording the master magnetic final mix. If the print is faulty a new one must be made.

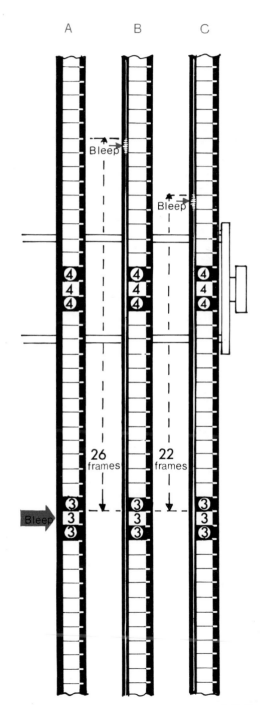

Out-of-sync comopt copies
The sync bleep, originally on three of the magnetic leaders, is advanced by 26 frames on comopt print (B) showing that in this instance sound and picture negatives have been correctly synchronised for printing. Comopt print (C) is out of sync. The sound has only been advanced 22 frames. Sync bleeps provide an instant sync check on comopt copies.

139

Picture Faults

If shots on the answer print are too dark or too light either the grader has picked the wrong light for the shot or the printing machine has missed its cue at the start of the shot. Again, the remedy lies with the laboratory. Ask the laboratory to check, and give them exact details of the scenes you are not happy with. If the whole print is too light or too dark the trouble may be due to faulty processing. Again, the faults are not cutting faults.

Prints from out of sync A & B rolls

If the answer print contains black frames the fault may well be in the cutting room. The A and B rolls of the camera original may be out of sync. Clear, flash frames can also be caused by the same fault. The remedy is to wind through A and B rolls of the original in a synchroniser and check each cut against the cutting copy. If the A and B rolls are out of sync you will find dissolves occur in the wrong places in your answer print. Again, the remedy is to check the camera original in the synchroniser. If the rolls are out of sync, adjust the spacing, joining in more frames or removing them, as necessary, until the two rolls compliment each other. You will then have to reprint and, if you neg cut the film and send the A and B rolls in out of sync, you will have to pay for the reprint.

Other print faults

What other print faults may you find? Perhaps you are expecting to see a fade at a particular point and it has not been produced on the answer print. Did you remember to tell the laboratories where you wanted the fade? If you did not provide instructions when you sent the edited camera original for grading you should not expect to see the fades produced in your print. Small white dots might also appear from time to time — sometimes there are so many they look like a small snowstorm. This fault is known as sparkle and it is usually caused by loose specks of dirt on the camera original. The remedy is to clean the original and reprint.

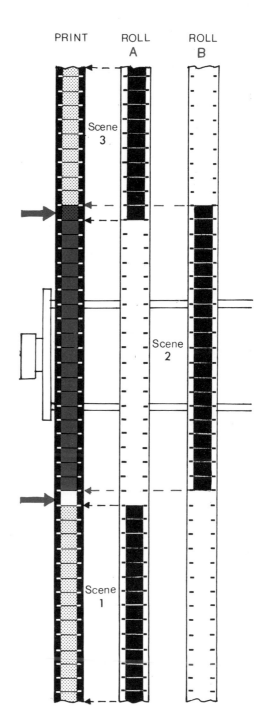

PRINT   ROLL   ROLL
         A   B

Scene 3

Scene 2

Scene 1

Check print against originals
The negative cutter has cut one frame too soon at the end of scene 1 leaving a frame of black spacing which shows as a clear (flash) frame on the print. At the cut from scene 2 to 3 he has left one frame too many on roll A giving a double frame of one frame at that point. The remedy is to adjust the A/B rolls by cutting in the spacing between the shots, check again and then reprint.

Faults Difficult to Remedy

When you are checking a print, scratches may also become apparent. They can be a serious fault and a difficult one to remedy. First check that they are not on the print itself. When you have run the print right through, wind back to the scene where you saw the scratch and hold it against a strong light slightly bending the film. You will see the physical marks of scratches on either base or the emulsion side of the material. Bend the film slowly, letting light fall directly across it until you can see the scratch marks. If they are on the print this method of testing will find them. If the original is scratched they will be much more difficult to see. Scratches are always a problem to remedy. Print scratches are often best remedied by re-printing. If a scratch is on the base side of the original, polishing may remove it. If on the emulsion side it will be more difficult to get rid of, though polishing can sometimes prove effective. Ask the laboratory to check the scratches and to investigate the possibilities of polishing them out. Emulsion scratches are often impossible to remove.

Edge fogging

You may occasionally find that some parts of a colour film are edge-fogged. This usually happens when a colour film has been cut in black and white. If the black and white cutting copy was not made on panchromatic stock, edge fogging will often not be apparent until a colour print is produced. If your answer print contains fogged shots there is only one remedy — replace the shot with an alternative shot or take. Of course, before you make any replacements you must check the print and the camera original. It may be the print stock which is fogged.

Complaining to a laboratory

In all these matters, as indeed in so much of the cutting process, it is important to work closely with the processing laboratory. A working relationship which really does work must be established from the very beginning. If you find that your print has a fault in it, make sure the fault is not your own before you complain to the processing lab.

PRINT FAULTS

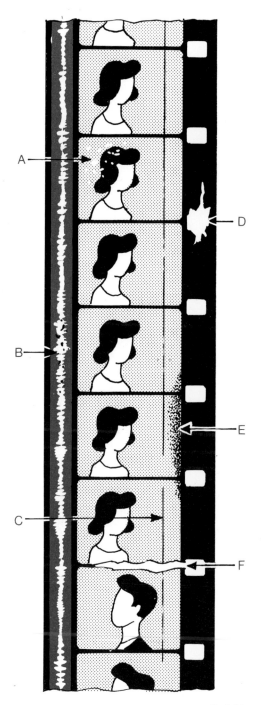

Types of fault among common print faults
you will find: (A) Sparkle (if it is white it is probably dust on the neg), (B) Dirt on the sound track, (C) A scratch. (D) Torn perforation, (E) Edge fogging, (F) Torn join. Check the print and the original and make sure the fault is not your own before complaining to the laboratory.

143

Safeguarding Original: Dupe Masters

If you expect to make a number of copies of your film you should prepare duplicate master materials so that you do not wear out the original by making a large number of prints.

Making multiple copies
The camera original (the master film from which your answer print was made) will not last for ever. It can be scratched, it can get dirty and if it is used frequently it will become worn. And, remember, when the original is damaged that damage will be reproduced on every print. So, duplicate master materials are essential if more than a few prints are to be produced. Check your answer print and if it is perfect, ask the laboratory to make a dupe. They will make it in the same way as they make a print, by re-exposing one piece of film (the original or the master) on another (a duplicate master). Sometimes an intermediate positive stage is needed, as the diagrams on the following pages show.

Colour reversal internegative
If the original film was shot on Eastmancolor negative it is quite possible to make a duplicate negative in one stage. The laboratory load one side of their printing machine with the original cut negative and the other side with a reel of unexposed reversal internegative stock. The original is re-exposed and the new reversal internegative processed. It can then be used for making subsequent prints. Colour reversal internegatives are usually referred to by the letters CRI.

Advantages and disadvantages of dupe masters
The quality of the duplicate master is never quite as good as an original, though if the original is up to professional standards the difference should only be marginal. Indeed Eastmancolor reversal internegative stock is so good that it is often difficult to tell the dupe from an original. The definition of the image can even appear to be sharper and the colours more saturated on a C.R.I. Duplicates do have some advantages. As there are no joins, there should be less wear and tear as the film passes through the printer. They are also replaceable whereas a cut original is not. If a dupe gets damaged or worn out you have only to go back to the master and make another dupe. Duplicates can be used for making numerous prints. The exact number you can make depends to some extent on the efficiency of the processing laboratory. If the film is handled carefully and modern equipment is used you should be able to make at least a hundred prints without signs of wear becoming apparent.

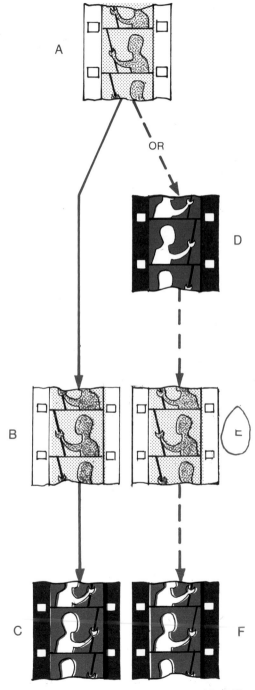

A

OR

D

B

E

Dupes of colour negative originals

You have two alternative methods to choose from. You either print the original colour negative (A) on colour interpositive (D) and then re-expose the interpositive on colour internegative stock (E). The internegative can then be used for printing.

Alternatively you can print (A) on to colour reversal internegative (B) and use the CRI to make prints. The latter system gives better quality results.

C

F

145

The Original: Neg and Pos Dupes

If the film has been shot on 16mm reversal, like Ektachrome, when you have a satisfactory answer print there are two courses you can follow if you want to make a dupe.

Dupes from Ektachrome originals

You can either make a duplicate reversal Ektachrome master or you can make a negative from the reversal original. To make a duplicate reversal master the laboratory simply re-expose the cut original on duplicate master reversal colour stock. Copies can then be made by printing the duplicate master on reversal stock. Alternatively, you can have the original cut colour master printed on colour negative stock, thus making a colour negative from which further copies can be made by printing on colour positive. If, for example, your film was shot on 16mm Ektachrome, you can either print the cut Ektachrome on dupe Ektachrome stock to make a master dupe and then print the processed master dupe on ordinary reversal colour stock to make subsequent prints, or you can print the cut Ektachrome original on Eastmancolor negative stock and then print the processed Eastman colour negative on Eastman colour positive stock to make your prints. The negative method has several advantages. It is usually cheaper to make prints by printing colour negative on colour positive than it is to print colour reversal on colour reversal, and contrast can be more accurately controlled.

Dupes from black and white originals

Preparing duplicates for 16mm films shot in black and white is also a simple process. For films shot on black and white negative a duplicate negative must be made. This cannot be done in one stage, like the colour negative process. An intermediate positive copy must be made. The original cut negative must be re-exposed on a low contrast fine grain positive stock, known as a fine grain dupe pos. The duping positive can then be developed and itself be re-exposed on a reel of duplicate negative stock. Copies of the film can then be made by printing the duplicate negative on black and white positive stock.

When an original is shot on 16mm black and white reversal there is again a choice of systems. A duplicate reversal master can be made by printing the cut reversal original on duplicate reversal stock. Copies can then be made by printing the dupe on other reversal stock. Alternatively the cut reversal original can be printed on negative stock. The processed negative can then be printed on positive film to make further copies. The neg/pos method has the advantage of making prints cheaper.

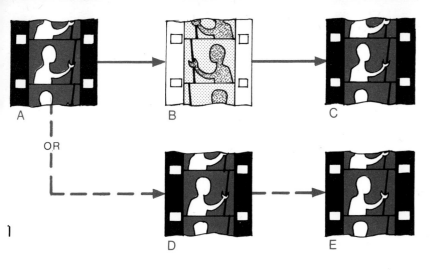

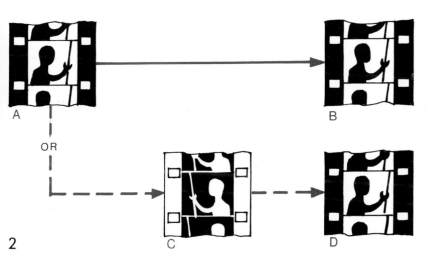

PROTECTING THE ORIGINAL

1. Colour reversal originals
From a colour reversal original (like Ektachrome) (A) you can make an Ektachrome dupe master (D) which can be used for making colour prints on reversal stock (E). Alternatively, you can make a colour internegative (B) which can then be printed on colour positive stock (C). The latter method enables you to produce copies at lower cost.

2. Black and white reversal originals (A) can be printed on black and white reversal stock (B) which can be used for making further copies on reversal stock. Alternatively, a black and white negative (C) can be made from the reversal original. The negative can then be printed on black and white positive stock (D). The latter system results in better and cheaper prints.

147

Moving from Gauge to Gauge

Your 16mm film may need to include 35mm shots and you may indeed want to make copies of the finished film available in another format. Are the gauges interchangeable?

35mm reduced to 16mm
35mm originals can be reduced to 16mm without problems. If the 35mm original is in colour, shot on Eastmancolor negative, you can either make a straight 16mm reduction print by asking the laboratory to re-expose the cut 35mm Eastmancolor negative on a roll of 16mm colour positive stock, or you can make a 16mm reversal internegative from the 35mm cut original and use the dupe for making 16mm copies. If you expect to make more than a couple of prints a 16mm dupe neg should be made. A 35mm black and white original can be reduced to 16mm by making a 35mm fine grain duping positive from the cut 35mm original negative and by subsequently re-exposing the 35mm dupe pos on 16mm black and white negative stock.

16mm enlarged to 35mm
Can 16mm be enlarged to 35mm? It is technically possible to enlarge 16mm to 35mm but the results are not always satisfactory. A 16mm Ektachrome colour reversal original can be enlarged to 35mm by print-ing the 16mm original on 35mm colour negative which can then itself be used to make subsequent 35mm prints. Eastman 16mm colour negative can be printed on 35mm colour reversal internegative stock. The CRI can then be used to make 35mm copies. Again, the diagram shows the stages involved in making these dupes.

16mm reduced to Super 8mm
16mm should only be enlarged to 35mm as a last resort. The quality is usually poor, 35mm originals can however be reduced to 16mm with complete confidence. 16mm films can also be reduced to Super 8mm without problems. When Super 8mm copies are required it is normally only practicable to make even numbers of prints. Few laboratories will produce single copies. If you want to make a number of Super 8mm prints, it is best to make a reduction dupe negative on Super 8mm stock.

Conclusion
When you have prepared duplicate master materials so that copies of the film you have cut can be produced, you have finished your work. You started with reels of rushes. You have finished a film which will hold the attention of an audience. And that's what cutting is all about.

148

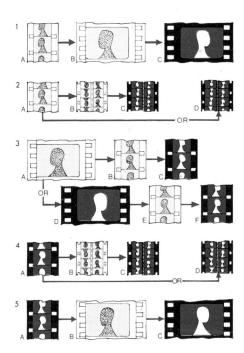

INTERCHANGING FORMATS

1. 16mm colour negative
Can be "blown up" to 35mm colour reversal internegative (B).).

2. 16mm colour negative
Can be printed on super 8mm colour interneg (B) from which contact super 8mm colour prints can be made on colour positive stock (C). Alternatively, the 16mm colour neg can be directly reduction printed on to super 8mm colour positive (D). The former system is normally used when more than two prints are needed.

3. 35mm colour negative
Can either be reduction printed on 16mm colour reversal internegative (B) from which 16mm colour contact prints can be made (C) or it can be contact printed on 35mm colour interpositive (D). The 35mm interpositive can then be reduction printed on a 16mm internegative (E) from which 16mm contact colour prints can be produced (F).

4. 16mm reversal colour originals
Can be printed on super 8mm colour interneg (B) which can then be used to make super 8mm colour contact prints (C), or it can then be used to make super 8mm colour reversal stock (D).

5. 16mm reversal colour originals
(A) can be enlarged ("blown up") on to 35mm colour internegative (B). The internegative can be used for making 35mm colour contact prints (C).

Film Running Times (16mm)

Feet	at 24 f.p.s.		at 25 f.p.s.	
	Min.	Sec.	Min.	Sec.
1		1·7		1·6
2		3·3		3·2
3		5·0		4·8
4		6·7		6·4
5		8·3		8·0
6		10·0		9·6
7		11·7		11·2
8		13·3		12·8
9		15·0		14·4
10		16·7		16·0
20		33·3		32·0
30		50·0		48·0
40	1	6·7	1	4·0
50	1	23·0	1	20·0
60	1	40·0	1	36·0
70	1	57·0	1	52·0
80	2	13·0	2	8·0
90	2	30·0	2	24·0
100	2	47·0	2	40·0
200	5	33·0	5	20·0
300	8	20·0	8	—
400	11	6·0	10	40·0
500	13	53·0	13	20·0
600	16	40·0	16	—
700	19	30·0	18	40·0
800	22	12·0	21	20·0
900	25	—	24	—
1000	27	46·0	26	40·0
2000	55	32·0	53	20·0

Further Reading

BADDELEY, W, HUGH:
The Technique of Documentary Film Production. Focal Press, London, and Hastings House, New York 1975
A discussion on the whole range of documentary film production techniques including basic advice on cutting.

BURDER, JOHN:
The Technique of Editing 16mm Film. Focal Press, London, and Hastings House, New York 1971
A detailed exploration of the basic and finer points of editing 16mm films from rushes to answer print.

BURDER, JOHN:
Work of the Industrial Film Maker. Focal Press, London, and Hastings House, New York 1973
A comprehensive study of the techniques involved in planning and making industrially sponsored films showing the importance of cutting in the film production programme.

HAPPÉ, BERNARD:
Your Film and the Lab. Focal Press, London, and Hastings House, New York 1974
The laboratory's contribution to film making is examined in depth.

REISZ, KAREL and MILLAR, GAVIN:
The Technique of Film Editing. Focal Press, London, and Hastings House, New York 1968
A study of the artistic aspects of film cutting. Interesting when the basic techniques have been mastered.

STONE, VERNON and HINSON, BRUCE:
Television Newsfilm Techniques. Focal Press, London and Hastings House, New York 1974
A basic source of information on US newsfilm practices in TV news operations in which 16mm film is used primarily.

WALTER, ERNEST:
The Technique of the Film Cutting Room. Focal Press, London, and Hastings House, New York 1973
The activities of the feature film editor and his assistants working with 35 mm film are outlined and discussed.

Glossary

A/B Rolls (92) (140) A negative cutting system. Cut master material is assembled in two rolls with scenes alternating from roll to roll at dissolves or wipes. The system enables optical effects to be printed from original master material in one stage thus ensuring optimum quality copies.

Academy Leader (6) A precise length of film carrying identification and projection operation information which is attached to the head of reels of sound and/or picture.

Acmade Miniola (18) A low cost 16mm editing machine enabling 16mm picture to be edited with one separate 16mm magnetic soundtrack.

Animated Viewer (32) A small viewing device usually employing a rotating prism to back project a picture on a small screen. Though not suitable for creative editing work, viewers can sometimes be useful for locating material.

Answer Print (136) (140) (142) The first graded ("timed" in the USA) show print is often known as an answer print.

Big Close Up (abbreviated BCU) (38) Shot framing only a small part of a subject, closer than a close up (CU), part of a human face for example.

Blow Up (148) The technique of making a larger picture copy of a film shot on a smaller gauge material. A 35mm copy of a film shot on 16mm is known as a 'blow up'.

Camera Original (See **Master**).

Camera Sheets (40) Information sheets completed during filming, specifying the type of film stock used and providing the laboratory with processing instructions and the editor with exact details of every scene and take filmed.

Checkerboard (86) (87) (140) A negative cutting system similar to A/B rolls in which master material is assembled in two rolls enabling optical effects to be printed directly from the original. In a checkerboard assembly, scenes alternate from roll to roll at every cut, whereas in an ordinary A/B roll they only alternate at dissolves or wipes.

Chinagraph Grease pencils used for marking cutting points and other symbols on base side of film.

Cinex Strips (46) A series of individual frames printed at a range of exposures as a grading test. In a black and white film each frame is printed at different printer light increasing from very light to very dark. In a colour original, the density gradation is replaced by a gradation of colour filter selections.

Clapper Board (120) Frequently referred to as a slate, a clapper board consists of two pieces of board hinged together in such a way that the two parts of the board can be banged together at the start of a synchronised sound take. Scene and take numbers are written on the board so that the action can be later idetified. The film editor matches the point where the two pieces of the board actually bang together, with the corresponding bang on the soundtrack and is thus able to synchronise sound and picture.

Close Up (38) (Abbreviated to CU). Shot taken, close in effect, to a subject, revealing detail. In the case of a human subject, a shot of the face only or the hands only, would be classified as a close up.

Combined Print (132) (134) A print where the soundtrack and action are printed together on the same piece of film stock. Also known as a married print. Prints with combined optical soundtracks are known as "comopt" copies and prints with a combined magnetic sound stripe are known as "commag".

Commentary (124) (126) Spoken words accompanying a film. The speaker usually remains unseen. Also known as **Narration and Voice Over.**

Continuity (64) (66) The flow from one shot to another without breaks or discrepancies. Smoothness in the development of subject matter.

Colour Master (44) Original colour film exposed in the camera.

Core (centre) A plastic core on which film is sometimes wound. In a cutting room film is usually handled on cores rather than on reels with fixed sides. (See **Split Spool**).

Cutaway (68) A shot of something other than the main theme of the action. A cutaway is inserted between shots of the main action, often to bridge a time lapse or to avoid a jump cut.

Cutting Copy (48) (80) Often abbreviated simply as C/C, and sometimes referred to as a **Workprint,** the cutting copy is the name given to the print used for editing purposes. Rushes when edited become the cutting copy.

Cutting Ratio (54) The amount of film used in the final edited version in relation to the amount shot. For example a ratio of 10 : 1 means ten times more film was shot than used.

Dailies (See **Rushes**)

Dissolve (70) An optical effect in which one scene gradually replaces another. In essence a fade out and a fade in are superimposed. Also known as a **Mix.**

Double System (100) A system of sound recording used for shooting synchronised sound takes. Sound is recorded on separate magnetic film or on $\frac{1}{4}$in tape and not (as in the single system) on the edge of the actual film in the camera.

Double Take (66) Continuity errors in which the same action is incorrectly allowed to be seen twice.

Dubbing (128) (130) The name given to the various processes involved in re-recording a series of different separate magnetic soundtracks to make one final mixed soundtrack. Also the name given to re-voicing a film in another language.

Dupe (74) (146) (148) duplicated. A dupe negative is a duplicate (copy) negative and not the actual film exposed in the camera.

Edge Numbers (50) Numbers marked on the side of original film and thus on every copy made on a printer printing via a full gate. The numbers are used to match camera original material to an edited cutting copy when the work of cutting has been completed. If edge numbers are missing or are indistinct, ink numbers can be printed on both the original and the copy before cutting starts. Also known as key numbers.

Editor (10) The man (or woman) who does the cutting.

Emulsion The side of the film coated with light sensitive materials in the case of picture stock. The side of a magnetic sound track coated with ferrous oxide. Easily identified in either case by being the least shiny of the two sides.

Fade In (76) Gradual emergence of a shot out of darkness.

Fade Out (76) A shot that gradually disappears into complete darkness.

Film Bin (34) Large receptacle, often made of fibre and usually lined with a linen bag, into which film is allowed while shots are being assembled. In the USA film barrel or cutting barrel are the usual terms.

Final Mix (128) (130) The final composite soundtrack containing all music, dialogue, commentary and sound effects. The soundtrack the audiences hear.

Frame A single picture on a length of cine film or the corresponding amount of a perforated magnetic soundtrack. The lines dividing a picture into frames horizontally are known as frame lines.

Freeze Frame (76) The technique of freezing action so continuous movement stops and one individual frame remains on the screen as long as desired. Sometimes called a stop frame.

Gang Synchroniser (See **Synchroniser**).

Grading ("Timing" in the USA) (46) (136) Estimating the amount of light which must be allowed to pass through the individual scenes of a film when a copy is printed. In grading a colour film the laboratory grader will also have to assess the colour correction filters required to ensure colour balance from scene to scene. Though still a job which depends ultimately on the skill of a technician, modern equipment like the Haseltine colour analiser is now available to help with the work.

Inter-negative (146) A duplicate colour negative (i.e. not the original exposed in the camera). In the USA the term inter-negative refers primarily to a colour negative derived from a colour reversal original while other negatives are known as (colour dupe negatives).

Jump Cut (68) A cut which breaks the continuity by omitting an interval of time, revealing persons or objects in different positions in two adjacent shots.

Key numbers (See **Edge Numbers**).

"Laying" Sound (106) (110) (111) (112) (114) (116) Placing sound in the correct relationship with picture.
Leader (60) Blank film consisting of a coated or uncoated base, used as spacing when building up separate tracks of perforated magnetic film, and also used to provide additional protection at the head and end of reels. (See **Also Academy Leaders**).
Level Cut (**"Straight Cut"** or in the USA **"Editorial Cut"**). A cut where sound and picture are cut at the same point.
Library Shot (also known as a **Stock Shot**) (82) Shot used in a film but not taken specifically for it; shot taken from a film or library source outside the actual unit producing a film.
Loop (118) Short length of film or of magnetic soundtrack joined at its ends to form an endless loop so that it can be projected repetitively either to enable actors to fit words to lip movements (in the case of a picture loop) or to reproduce one sound continuously (in the case of magnetic sound loops).

Master (10) The original film exposed in the camera is the picture master. A master magnetic sound recording is an original recording from which other copies can be made.
Magnetic Stripe (132) Magnetic coating on the side of film used for magnetic recording.
Married Print A print combining sound and picture (see also **Combined Print**).
M & E (130) Widely used abbreviation for a mixed soundtrack of **Music and Sound Effects.** M & E tracks must be free of voice-over commentary though they should always contain synchronised dialogue scenes. M & E tracks are essential if foreign language versions are required. They are sometimes referred to as **"I.T. Band"** in European countries.
Medium Shot (Abbr. M.S.) (38) A shot taken at normal viewing distance, usually cutting actors at the waistline.
Miniola (18) (22) (See **Acmade Miniola**).

Mix (See **Dissolve**).

Moviola (18) (20) The trade name of a particular kind of motor driven upright editing machine usually equipped to run one reel of picture with one reel of separate perforated magnetic sound. In the USA the name has been in use for so many years that the term 'moviola' is widely used to describe motorised editing machines of any kind.

Narration (See **Commentary**).

Negative (44) (96) A piece of film where the tone values of the image are reversed. In the case of monochrome film negative, black appears as white and white as black.

Negative Cutting (84) (86) (88) (90) (92) (94) The matching of camera original film to an edited cutting copy.

Negative Cutter (12) (84) The person who matches original and cutting copy.

Optical Dupe Duplicate picture materials produced in the course of preparing optical effects. (See **Optical Effects**).

Optical Effects (70) (72) (74) (76) (78) (90) (96) Dissolves, fades in and out and other special effects like "freeze frames" are known as optical effects or simply as "opticals".

Optical Sound (132) (134) A photographic soundtrack, printed usually from an optical sound negative. Sound modulations are visible.

Panchromatic Stock (12) (48) Black and white film stock which is sensitive to all the colours of the spectrum. Widely used for making black and white copies of colour originals. The most practical advantage from an editor's point of view is that edge fogging can be seen, and thus avoided.

Picture Synchroniser (See **Synchroniser**).

Reversal Film (44) (96) A type of film stock which, after exposure and processing produces a positive image.

Release Print Projection print of the finished film, produced after the first graded (answer) print has been approved.

Rough Cut (62) The first assembly of picture and sound. In a rough cut scenes are put in script order for the first time but are often left over length.

Rushes (10) (40) (52) (54) (120) Copies of the film exposed in the camera made immediately after the original has been processed. Designed principally for cutting purposes, rushes are often printed ungraded. Also known in the USA as "dailies".

Show Print A graded copy of the finished film ready for projection.

Single System (102) A system of sound recording used for synchronised sound shooting. Sound is recorded on a magnetic stripe on the edge of the actual film in the camera. For rush work, like television news coverage, the processed original can be cut using the sound on the magnetic stripe. Alternatively, when the original has been processed, the sound on the stripe can be re-recorded on separate perforated magnetic film. If you cut with the mag stripe remember the sound will be 28 frames ahead of the picture to which it refers. If you re-record on sepmag stock you can edit in level synch, and thus enjoy more cutting freedom.

Sound Report Sheets (42) Information sheets completed by the sound recordist during filming noting the recording system used and the speed at which the sound was recorded. The sheets also provide transfer instructions for re-recording the masters on perforated magnetic film for cutting. Precise details of each scene and take number are also noted on the sheets.

Spacing (See **Leader**).

Split Spool (Also known as Split Reel). Reel with one detachable side. Film cores can be mounted on the reel and secured by replacement and locking of the flange. (See **Core**).

Steenbeck A range of table editing machines made in Germany.

Stock Shot (See **Library Shot**).

Stretch Printing (78) The optical printing process for making dupes of old film shot at silent film speeds and required for use in films shot at present day sound speeds. The jerkiness of the action can be evened out by printing every second frame twice.

Synchronisation (14) (104) (120) (122) (138) The precise marriage of sound and picture so that the sounds heard on the soundtrack exactly complement the pictures seen on the screen.

Synchroniser (Also known as a **Gang Synchroniser**) (24) (26) (54) Device used for maintaining synchronism between two or more pieces of film and consisting of two or more sprockets fixed to a common revolving shaft. Film placed on the sprockets can be moved forward or backwards whilst maintaining the synchronous relationship between the different pieces of film. Synchronisers are often fitted with magnetic sound heads and on some models the picture is back-projected on a small screen (Picture Synchronisers). One of the most important items of equipment in the cutting room. (See also **Negative Cutting and Track Laying**).

Wild Tracks (104) Sound recorded otherwise than with a synchronised picture. Wild tracks are normally used for random dialogue and background sound effects. Sometimes referred to as "non-sync".

Wipe Optical effect which provides the transition from scene to scene at the boundary of a line moving across the image until the incoming scene has entirely replaced the outgoing one. Wipes are not now very widely used.

Work Print Another name for the cutting copy.